AN INNER STEP TOWARD

GOD

WRITINGS AND TEACHINGS ON PRAYER BY
FATHER ALEXANDER MEN

EDITED AND INTRODUCED BY APRIL FRENCH
TRANSLATED BY CHRISTA BELYAEVA

PARACLETE PRESS
BREWSTER, MASSACHUSETTS

2014 First Printing

An Inner Step Toward God: Father Alexander Men's Writings and Teachings on Prayer

Copyright © 2014 by The Alexander Men Foundation (Russia)

ISBN 978-1-61261-238-6

Translated with permission from The Alexander Men Foundation, Moscow.

This book is a translation of major selections from:
Protoierei Aleksandr Men'. *Prakticheskoe rukovodstvo k molitve*. Second expanded edition, with the blessing of His Eminence Yuvenaly, the Metropolitan of Krutitsk and Kolomna. Moscow: Fond imeni Aleksandra Menia, 1995.

The Paraclete Press name and logo (dove on cross) are trademarks of Paraclete Press, Inc.

Library of Congress Cataloging-in-Publication Data is available.

10 9 8 7 6 5 4 3 2 1

Published by Paraclete Press
Brewster, Massachusetts
www.paracletepress.com

Printed in the United States of America

CONTENTS

FATHER ALEXANDER MEN
AND PRAYER

F ATHER ALEXANDER MEN (1935–1990) WAS A RUSSIAN
Orthodox priest in three parishes outside Moscow from 1960
to 1990. He wrote and spoke this book into being during the
last fifteen years of his life.

Despite many dangers, Father Alexander maintained a ministry
in the Soviet Union during the rules of Nikita Khrushchev, Leonid
Brezhnev, Yuri Andropov, Konstantin Chernenko, and Mikhail
Gorbachev. The KGB (Soviet secret police) and the Council for
Religious Affairs often called him in for interrogation, especially
during the Brezhnev and Andropov years. Only in the last three years
of his life was he able to take advantage of newfound freedoms under
Gorbachev's *glasnost* (openness) to lecture to thousands of people in
halls across Moscow and to speak on radio and television. He felt an
urgent need to communicate the gospel message to people before the
authorities were to clamp down on religious freedoms once again.
Father Alexander was murdered on September 9, 1990. His murder is
still unsolved, but many consider him a martyr.

A self-taught religious scholar at a time when works of a religious
nature were scarce and often illegal, Father Alexander published
many of his books under pseudonyms. Through his writings, he
intended to draw his fellow Soviet citizens to consider faith in
Christ. Throughout the late Soviet period, people circulated his
books through the clandestine literature networks of *samizdat* (self-

published, carbon-copied manuscripts) and *tamizdat* (books published abroad and smuggled back to the USSR). His key works include a life of Christ entitled *The Son of Man* (*samizdat* 1958, *tamizdat* 1968) and a six-volume work on ancient world religions up to the time of Christ, *In Search of the Way, the Truth, and the Life* (*samizdat* 1960–1969; *tamizdat* 1970–1983).[1] These works are a *tour de force* of scholarly erudition, making use of both older, respected sources and some of the most recent scholarship available in the world at the time.

In addition to scholarly works, Father Alexander wrote works of spiritual instruction for Orthodox believers, many of whom were new to the faith. His three-part series Life in the Church includes writings on the Church, Scripture, and prayer.[2] *A Practical Guide to Prayer*, the second section of the book you now hold, was intended as the third in this series, but it also functions as a stand-alone, instructional guide.

In the late 1970s, Father Alexander created a network for his parishioners to meet on a regular basis in various parts of Moscow to study Scripture and biblical history. This model resembled the "small groups" that developed in some Western church circles around the same time. In the Soviet Union, however, such gatherings were illegal, so participants needed to be careful to stagger their arrivals and exits from their hosts' apartments, so as not to arouse suspicion. A few of these small groups gathered specifically to learn more about prayer. They utilized the original manuscript version of *A Practical Guide to Prayer* in the late 1970s and early 1980s. The book was not actually published until 1991, the year after Father Alexander's untimely death. The version here translated is the second expanded edition from 1995, which also includes some of Father Alexander's lectures, informal talks, and sermons—all of which were tape-recorded and later transcribed.[3]

Throughout the text, you will encounter clues that point to the book's original Soviet context. Father Alexander wrote with a

Russian-speaking and Orthodox audience in mind. As you will see, however, this book contains much that is spiritually beneficial for any Christian, whether new to the faith or a seasoned person of prayer. Although Father Alexander was writing from a thoroughly Russian perspective, he was a good bridge between East and West. Through his style of expression, his respect for the Western Church, and his scholarship, many of his writings reflect a spirit of cooperation and a willingness to learn from Christians of other confessions. It is not surprising, therefore, that his writings are still popular among Christians of other confessions in Russia and beyond, as well as among certain circles of Russian Orthodox believers.[4] Even spiritual seekers find Father Alexander's writing appealing. During his lifetime in the Moscow area, he was always considered highly approachable. His writing style reflects that accessibility, and his books helped many Soviet citizens (and continue to help many Russian speakers around the world) on their journey to faith and spiritual maturity.

Among the myriad books already published about prayer, there are several factors that make this one unique. First, Father Alexander has a gift of presenting his erudition in a simple, accessible way. In doing so, he offers practical, step-by-step advice on deepening one's prayer life. Second, he highlights the participation of one's psychosomatic nature (body and soul) while praying from the prayer book, in order to facilitate spiritual union with God. Third, the book provides exposure to prayers not commonly used in the West. As you read, you will acquire a unique glimpse into the Christian life and practice within Soviet Russia and, we hope, you will find in Father Alexander a true spiritual director with a deep and abiding faith in Jesus Christ.

This book originated in Father Alexander's own practice of prayer. In addition to his regular prayer rule, and often after having led an early morning matins service, he prayed every morning at 9 AM in deep intercession for his parishioners and his "spiritual children" who lived throughout the world.[5] He invited some of them to set aside that time as well, so they could "commune" in prayer together from a distance.[6] While spiritually instructing new believers or people who were not yet believers, he wrote them letters to encourage their early attempts at prayer.[7] He also corresponded with seasoned believers, providing exhortation for deepening their prayer. As you read, you will notice that Father Alexander took great delight in learning about prayer from the Christian tradition—whether from the early Church Fathers, from spiritual writers in the Russian and Eastern Orthodox Church, or from Western writers.

Father Alexander always viewed humanity through the lens of "encounter." He believed that every person exists to have a personal encounter (*vstrecha*, also translated as *meeting*) with God, and that such encounters take place all the time. Many people, of course, do not realize that God is right there with them. Thus, they must learn to recognize their connection with God and to allow it to deepen and grow.[8]

His ministry is best summed up with three words: *courage, integrity,* and *presence*. For the majority of his service to the Russian Orthodox Church, Father Alexander faced opposition to his message—whether from the atheistic Soviet state, anti-Semites (Father Alexander was born into a Jewish family and baptized as an infant along with his mother, who had recently converted), the press, or anti-religious Soviet citizens—yet, he continued to courageously preach the Good News of Jesus through his written and spoken ministry. His integrity is evident in that he lived what he wrote. He was a man who had a vital personal relationship with and deep trust in God. Despite his busy (at times, frenetic) schedule, he set aside regular time for focused prayer. His faith informed every aspect of his life and ministry. Many who knew him have attested to having felt highly valued when they were in his presence. Father Alexander was fully present to people and met people where they were.

Daily life in the Soviet Union brought great stress, including overcrowded commutes, long lines for food, and (until the 1970s or 1980s) a lack of timesaving appliances for household tasks. Father Alexander knew that any guidance he would offer must be eminently practical and feasible if people were to grow in their relationship with God. This book reflects his penchant for a practical spirituality, something that is no less important in today's high-paced world.

Finally, a few words about the composition of this book. *An Inner Step Toward God* is a collection of many of Father Alexander Men's written and spoken communications on the subject of prayer, as well as some of his own prayers. Part I offers the reader a foundational understanding of the author's heart for prayer, setting the tone for the entire work. In the first chapter, which was taken from an informal talk in the home of a parishioner, Father Alexander mentions an essential ingredient for prayer—*an inner step* of deep faith, reliance, and trust in God despite difficult external circumstances. The second chapter, taken from a formal lecture, describes prayer as a response of love for and a sacramental encounter with the Lord.

Part II contains the work *A Practical Guide to Prayer*, written by Father Alexander and utilized by his small groups. He wrote it with a catechetical purpose in mind, which explains its rather didactic nature. The period of Great Lent is the focus of part III, which includes a sermon on the prayer of Saint Ephrem of Syria and an instructional guide on devotional practice during this crucial fast in the Christian calendar. The three chapters in part IV are bound together by the common theme of prayer within the communion of saints. Chapter twelve includes selections from Father Alexander's sermons on various saints; chapter thirteen provides a collection of public prayers spoken by Father Alexander, who is himself a part of "so great a cloud of witnesses" (Hebrews 12:1). Finally, chapter fourteen includes further selections from his sermons and lectures concerning prayer for others and prayer following the example of saints such as the Apostle Paul and Gregory of Palamas.

The appendices offer further insight from Father Alexander, as well as a few Orthodox prayers mentioned in the text. Ecclesiastical terms that may be unfamiliar to a Western Christian (e.g., *Theotokos* and *analoy*) are available in a glossary in the back. In addition, you will find a glossary with biographical information of important figures mentioned by Father Alexander. Should you encounter any questions concerning translation or format, please consult the notes from the translator and editor at the back of the book.

As he mentions in the introduction to *A Practical Guide to Prayer*, Father Alexander envisioned that people would read this work slowly and meditatively and would return to its pages over and over as they progressed in deepening their life of prayer. May the Lord bless your reading and your prayer life through Father Alexander's words of wisdom. As you ruminate on his guidance and put it into practice, may you take an inner step toward God and encounter Him anew.

PART ONE
AN INNER STEP

CHAPTER ONE

AN INNER STEP

ເວວ

Father Alexander often visited parishioners' homes, where small groups of people would gather to hear him speak (thus attracting less attention from the Soviet authorities). They called these times besedy *(conversations). This chapter is a transcribed talk given during one of these conversations sometime in the late 1970s or early 1980s, during the interval between Pascha (Easter) and Pentecost.*

W E EACH HAVE OUR OWN EXTERNAL AND INTERNAL reasons for the tiredness that has built up within us. We hope that our situation will somehow radically change when vacation comes. This hope is in vain, however, because we have already been on vacation numerous times and have continued to hobble along in the same way. In some ways, the times we live in are wonderful and happy. I do not regret that I live in this century. Yet, for *homo sapiens*, these times are a difficult trial, and even more so for those of us who live in a big city. This means that tension weighs upon us like a rock.

So, what can we do? There are all kinds of recommendations, including activities like autogenic training.[9] I have studied them practically and theoretically and have discovered that only one who has an abundance of free time can practice these somewhat beneficial methods. Overall, it is very complicated to determine which unknown factors may be weighing on us. We know that certain factors come from our genetic inheritance, and others come from the constant conflicts that arise at work and at home.

For us, *natural* ways of regeneration or revitalization are weak or hardly work at all. Therefore, I want to remind you of something that you already know well without my telling you. There are *supernatural* ways. Our spirit can receive more strength and overcome our soul's sluggishness and weakness only with the help of a lever. To access this lever, we do not need special methods of concentration or a long period of time, as with autogenic training. We do, however, need four things:

1. Six to ten minutes per day for prayers from the prayer book, which we read regardless of our mood. I am speaking of minimums here.
2. The same amount of time for the reading of the Gospels and the Holy Scriptures.
3. The Eucharist.
4. Prayerful fellowship with God.

Four things. This is not a theory. It has been tested practically.

Many people who have come to me with this common spiritual weakness of fatigue and tension tell me, "I have not done any of that." At that moment, I do not know what to tell them. It is as if a doctor had told someone that they had liver disease and that they should not eat fatty or salty food. If the patient were to come back and say, "Doctor, every day I eat bacon and salted herring," the doctor would just throw up his hands.

Specific methods give specific results. These practices have existed for centuries, a millennium, two millennia, or more. But it is important to keep all four elements. Nonetheless, we must remind ourselves that neither the gift of God, nor His grace and blessing are remedies or some kind of medicine. If this were the case, our egocentrism and demands on God would be in the forefront. We would not want to be something for Him, but would want Him to be something for us—a servant of some kind. Nothing good can come from this arrangement. Here, a huge *inner step* is necessary.

In one of Byron's tragedies, there is a description of a flood. A man recites a soliloquy on top of a cliff. He trusts God so much that, even if everything were covered in water, he would still die in absolute reliance on Him.[10] This man took an inner step of faith. Perhaps you feel that we lack accurate information concerning immortality, but you sense that God's will exists and directs everything. How? You do not know. Perhaps you think that only in His all-directing will do we have meaning. Perhaps you believe that in this flood, we have significance only to the extent that we are joined to Him. If you think this way, you have also taken this inner step, and His mystery is in the forefront—the main thing.

Thus, we should not approach prayer by saying something like, "My head hurts, so I want to pray for it to stop hurting." It does happen that the headache stops, but all the same, this attitude is not right. Prayer is deeply needed, but keep in mind that an egocentric, demanding approach cannot be entirely correct. It is necessary to do something more, to seek not only for our own sakes. But this is already a further step.

There are three main types of prayer: *supplication* (our very favorite), *confession*, and *thanksgiving*. Supplication is blessed and commanded. We find it in the Lord's Prayer. Notice, however, that the Lord's Prayer begins not with supplication, but with acceptance and consent: "Thy kingdom come, Thy will be done." Only then does it say, "Give us this day our daily bread." You see, in this we find inner liberation. We are not free, and we must begin by freeing ourselves from everything, in order to straighten the shoulders of our souls that are bent under a heavy burden. Someone once said that if we were to fulfill just half of the Sermon on the Mount, all our complexes would pass. This is true. Something is always gnawing at us, gnawing continually. And this turns into an obsession: "I need to do this. I need to do that. Everything must be done." It becomes a hindrance rather than a benefit, because it turns into an obsessive idea against a difficult backdrop of anxiety. Remember that we are mortal, that life is short, and that the Lord said, "Do not worry about your life, what you will eat or what you will drink" (Matt. 6:25; see also Lk. 12:22). By this He meant that, even though the circumstances seem overwhelming, we must simply put one foot in front of the other and press on.[11] If we do make plans for the future, they must be nothing more than sketches, nothing that would enslave us.

We are free and happy despite the weaknesses that hold us down, because we participate in the mystery of God's grace, and many amazing and wonderful things are being revealed to us. In addition, we have many brothers and sisters. They are here, in church, around the entire city, all over the world. We are included in the Eternal Divine.

Another amazing thing is that we can look at everything—scientific formulas and any other phenomenon—through the prism of the Divine. This morning, I turned the television on and saw an octopus. It was a truly divine spectacle! Despite the fact that the show ended soon after I turned the television on, those few seconds brought me into a state of absolute elation. Any object can elicit awe. We must not lose our ability to look afresh at things, at our neighbors, at the world around us and to try to take life as it comes. It is easier to live if we know how to push oppressive situations away from ourselves when necessary, to rise above them and to become free sojourners. We are but sojourners. We are guests here, strangers. The Apostle Paul said that we are only sojourners on the earth, "strangers and pilgrims" (Heb. 11:13–14). In one of the apocryphal Gospels, the

Lord Jesus describes the world as a bridge; as you know, bridges exist to be crossed.[12]

In the Lord's Prayer, we begin speaking to the Father in heaven. Who is the Father? This is our relative, the One who is most closely related to us. And what does "in heaven" mean? It means that He is in another dimension of existence, our homeland. By homeland, I do not mean a place of physical birth or a place to which we are emotionally attached. This is a different thing altogether. It is a natural human tendency to be emotionally attached to one's neighborhood, home, language, city, or country, but there is another place that we call our homeland. It is difficult to describe. Mikhail Lermontov made an attempt in his famous poem about a soul that was brought to earth by an angel just as it was about to be born; the singing of angels remained forever inside this soul.[13] This is only an image, but a deep one, because we do have another homeland. Something ties us to the spiritual world. We are, therefore, guests here and are often uncomfortable in this world. We *should* be uncomfortable, because this world is full of crude material, "the whole world lies *under the sway of the wicked one*" (1 John 5:19). We collide with the world, and it wounds us. Is it not that much more important that we call on the Spirit? And the Spirit comes, especially when we are together. For this reason, we gather in church and pray together as well as we can.

The days of *Pascha* (Easter) are coming to an end, and as this time ends, it is as if we relive these events again. The resurrected Lord comes to us again, as He did on the road to Emmaus when he came to his disciples saying, "Peace to you" (Lk. 24:36; see also John 20:19). This phrase is not merely an ancient Hebrew greeting. Of course, He was greeting them, but He incorporated something else that was very deep. In ancient Hebrew, the word *shalom* (peace) means not only the absence of war, but also a particular state of blessedness, a particular state of peacefulness in the soul, and an intimacy with God. This is the peace that we ask from God. Peace with God and peace with each other.

So let us pray that we may know He is with us right now. The Word of God will be with us. We will take Him home, and He will live in us. And finally, let us live in the light and in hope. We believers are happy people who do not take advantage of our happiness; we are rich people who neither take possession of nor utilize our treasure. Therefore, today we will wash away everything—our resentments, our disappointments, our worries and expectations, our sins, and our burdens. We bring these things to the Lord so that He might strengthen us, for this is what is most important. And now let us pray . . .

 Lord Jesus Christ,
   In this evening hour,
   In this city where Your blessing is bestowed,
   In the midst of suffering and sin and tragedy,
   You who suffered
   And took upon Yourself the plague of humanity
   Because You loved us,
   You who have come here,
   Abide with us.

   Lord, You carried the Cross.
   Teach us to bear suffering
   And to labor for the sake of our neighbors.
   Lord Jesus Christ,
   You see our wounds and our weaknesses.
   Pour strength into us,
   Make us steadfast, courageous, and worthy witnesses
   Of Your Divine Gospel.

Lord Jesus Christ,
In these days that You have allotted to us,
Allow us to carry Your Cross as a banner.

Lord Jesus Christ, help us.
We thank You for all the miraculous things You give us
In nature, in the Church,
In the Sacraments, in Your Holy Scriptures,
In people's writings that are inspired by You,
In our neighbors, in our loved ones,
And in everything that fascinates us, excites us, and surprises us.

We thank You for all things, Lord.
Help us to be true bearers of Your Name.

Amen.

CHAPTER TWO
PRAYER
LOVING RESPONSE AND
SACRAMENTAL ENCOUNTER

In the late 1980s and early 1990s, an unprecedented public forum opened up in the Soviet Union, and Father Alexander took advantage of the opportunity to speak publicly about the Christian faith and religious history and philosophy. This chapter consists of a lecture, originally entitled "O molitve" ("On Prayer"), that he gave at the Kranaya Presnya Club in Moscow on February 3, 1990, just seven months before he was killed.

LET'S TALK ABOUT CHURCH PRACTICES AND WHAT IS manifest in the daily Christian life. In discussions about higher matters and the spiritual purpose of the entire creation, some initial questions may arise. Is it worthwhile to tie these higher matters to traditions, customs, and rituals? Are they all just "survivals" and tributes to times long past?[14] Is there really such a thing as "serving God"? How can people serve God? Does God have needs?

In reality, the Holy Scriptures give us the answer that Divine Love does need us. He needs a responsive act of our hearts. "My son, give me your heart" (Prov. 23:26). This means that our responsive love is our service to God. This love is in response to the work of the Creator in the world, in nature, and in the life of our hearts. But can our love be detached, only internal, or subjective? Of course not!

Why not? Because we are living beings; we are made of flesh and blood. Therefore, all our feelings and circumstances are inseparably bound to the life of our soul and body.

We must always remember that, speaking simplistically, a person consists of the spirit, the soul, and the body.[15] All of them are woven together. The state of your body will reflect directly on the state of your soul, and consequently on the state of your spirit. A person has a completely different attitude depending upon whether he is lounging, sitting, standing erect, or kneeling. The position of the body influences the state of the soul.

Let me give you just one example. In the late 1950s, I went to a Baptist service in Siberia. There, the accountant at our agricultural institute preached and told a story that would seem not to fit Baptist practice, since icons are not used in their worship.[16] In the story, a man stood before a remarkable icon—the work of an ancient master— depicting the Crucifixion. The man said, "What's so great about this icon? Maybe the paint is wonderful, and the artist shows mastery, but I do not feel any spiritual power." Then a girl standing nearby whispered to him, "Stand on your knees." And he was so moved by her comment that he did get on his knees before the image. Suddenly, everything was transfigured, and something particular opened up to him that he had not felt until that moment.

Everything connected with our life must be expressed outwardly. Consider the abundance of rituals in our everyday life, which has generally been rather stripped of rituals. Which ones have remained? Saluting in the military, shaking hands, waving good-bye to someone at a train platform, applauding—each of these is a ritual, a sign, a symbol. Many such symbols have lasted. A person, as a being made of flesh and blood, has the need to express his feelings outwardly. This is why the Church commands rituals. Christ the Savior observed rituals. Yet He warned that, as soon as we begin to give them too much significance and forget that they are but vessels for spiritual content, we descend into ritualism.

One of the simplest rituals, the sign of the cross, is connected to personal, individual prayer. According to Christian tradition (at least according to the ecclesiastical traditions of Catholicism and Orthodoxy), when a person prays, he crosses himself. Ultimately, this gesture is closely connected to prayerful concentration and to the prayerful state of the heart, of the body and its systems, and of the motor memory. This is why, when a person wants to pray (or when he is in a bad mood or is afraid), he crosses himself. This gesture helps him to get himself together to take an inner step toward God.

The Christian life cannot develop without prayer. People often approach me with the question, "How can I pray, since I do not know any prayers?" This, my friends, is a mistake, because when you talk to each other or to a loved one, you do not need to read a paper or seek someone else's words. It is not for nothing that we mock public officials who read everything from a script.[17] When a person speaks with someone, he should speak naturally, from his heart. Prayers written in the prayer book are just aids. They are not spells or pagan formulas that summon a spirit, but rather a conversation between a person and God—a sacramental, vivifying encounter that gives purpose, fullness of life, and incomparable joy. Prayer is the soul's encounter with its only Beloved, its only Savior. For this encounter to take place, a person must have his own words.

But it is easy enough to understand why the Church has given us the words and forms of prayer that have arisen through centuries in the practice of its ascetics. It is due to our spiritual ignorance, stagnation, and lack of enlightenment. It is because we so often bustle about that we cannot compose ourselves or concentrate for prayer. When we learn prayers from the prayer book by heart, we can put them into practice. I must emphasize that it is necessary to distinguish *prayer* from saying prayers from the prayer book. Prayer is the flight of the heart to God. Reading prayers from the prayer book is the pronunciation of prayer texts. In many churches, you can acquire a prayer book that contains morning, evening, and other prayers.

One of my Baptist friends said, "Perhaps you do not need those old words written by someone else. Relate to God in your own words." Was he right? Yes, of course. As our Creator Himself says, nothing is more valuable to Him than what comes directly from the heart. And when Christ gave the Lord's Prayer to His disciples, He surely did not just give a standard text that people must repeat. He said that we should not pray a bunch of formulas; only the heathen pray that way (see Matt. 6:7). Why the heathen, or pagans? Because a pagan was sure that with incantation, it was possible to force the deity to work for him by calling down rain or causing it to stop. In these mantras, there is a sort of competition with God, as if one were trying to take Him over and use Him for one's own purposes. Therefore, Christ asks us not to use many words in prayer, but to pray simply.

You should all remember this prayer: "Our Father, who art in heaven, hallowed be Thy name." This prayer does not begin with a petition that says, "Give me something." Some people think that prayer always asks for something. Love is not like that. If your children came to you only to get money, you would understand that they do not love you, but your money. True faith is directed primarily toward God, and only secondarily toward His gifts.

Thus, the Lord's Prayer first speaks of Him. "Hallowed be Thy name." In other words, "Lord, may You always be our sanctuary." "Name" in biblical language means "You Yourself." This is the holy specification of God Himself, the name of God. At one time, it was said that His name was in this or that place, which signified that His power was there. "Hallowed be" means, "May Your name always be a sanctuary for us, always most beloved and valued."

"Thy Kingdom come." This is the goal that God has inscribed on creation. "Thy will be done." These are divine words, the same words that Christ said in the prayer at the Garden of Gethsemane before His death. He spoke this prayer on the night when the sins of each one of us were upon Him like a rock; these sins crumbled when He said, "Not My will, but Yours, be done" (Lk. 22:42). The human and divine wills residing in Him crossed and collided, and Love was the victor: "Thy will be done."

How happy, how stable, how brave, how free is the one who is able to feel these words deep down inside and run them through his heart! "Thy will be done." Yet let us never forget that, in reality, we constantly come up against the exact opposite formula: "My will be done."

Perhaps God wants one thing, but I want another. I knew a young woman who wanted to do a certain thing and asked for a blessing. The priest said, "No, not under any circumstances." She was not hindered, but went to another priest whom she knew and asked him for a blessing. He said this was not ever allowed. But she did not give up. Since we are not on the North Pole and there are still many Orthodox churches and priests, she went to each one until she found someone to say, "Sure, no problem." Then she wrote me a joyous letter about how Father So-and-So blessed her to do such-and-such. Of course, I was a bit surprised, until later, upon hearing the story of her trek, I understood that she wanted to hear only one answer from the start. This was not a question, not a request. When you ask, expecting beforehand to get a particular answer, it is better not to ask at all, because in your heart is the phrase, "My will be done, by hook or by crook." Why did she go to all those priests? She did so simply to make herself feel better, so that later on, she could say that she had received a blessing to do it. Thus, it turned out that she won on two fronts: she got to do what she wanted and had supposedly received sanctions to do so. This self-deception is harmless when talking about insignificant things, but it can become sufficiently significant when speaking of more serious things. More importantly, this is a false mindset.

Of course, you may ask me, "How then can I know God's will?" Honestly, this question is, as a rule, deceptive and vacuous. In most cases, it will not be a riddle as to what God's will is if we seriously study the problem, if we know the Word of God well enough, and finally if, having prayed, we ask God. Undoubtedly, there are particular, extreme situations when it is difficult to discern, but exceptions only prove the rule. Actually, I have often seen in those cases when a person has said, "I don't know God's will," that once we have talked about it, it has turned out that he knew all along and just "played dumb."

Christ adds here: "Thy will be done on earth as it is in heaven." We should not think that the Creator's will is something otherworldly, that it is accomplished somewhere in another world or some time in the distant future. No, the Kingdom of God has already come; it already lives in this world and can come into each one of us. It can become a reality in each of our lives. The Lord wants His Kingdom to be here.

There is no need to search for the meaning of Christ's words, "My kingdom is not of this world" (John 18:36). Our popular expression "out of this world" tends toward dreams, abstraction, and fantasy. When we say that a person is "in another world," then in the best-case scenario, the person is oblivious to what is going on in this world. But Christ meant something very different from this. His Kingdom comes into the world from a different, higher dimension, but it enters into our world and into the details and kinks of our everyday life. That is why we say, "Thy will be done" both on earth and in heaven, in our personal lives, and even in society. To live any other way is impossible, because we are social beings.

When society is unjust, God's will is trampled upon and thrown out. We should not try to combine the highest divine purpose—God's Kingdom—with various political utopias, as was sometimes done in the 1920s.[18] When Hewlett Johnson, the Dean of Canterbury known as the "Red Priest," came to visit the USSR, he said that Christianity and communism shared a single goal—the happiness of man. In England, he spoke and wrote along those lines, claiming that Christ had set moral commandments, but Stalin had brought them to fruition.[19] This is a very shallow judgment that has nothing to do with reality.

The goal of the Kingdom of God is not some perfect political order. Yet, it is a challenge to God's will when evil and injustice rule in the world. Of course, the goal of Christianity is deeper and more all-encompassing than simply a political reconstruction (*perestroika*) in one area or another. The life of society can be described with the following metaphor: You cannot build a good, strong house out of bad stones or bricks that are breaking and crumbling. Similarly, you cannot build a society on the best of laws if the people themselves, the members of the society, are in a state of moral decline.

The will of Christ on earth is for both our societal life and our personal life, in the most intimate depths. And after a person says, "Thy will be done, Thy Kingdom, Thy Holiness," then he can begin to make requests like, "Give us this day our daily bread." What does this mean? It means we are asking Him to give us that which is necessary for our life. "Daily" in this case carries the connotation of being necessary. Why only necessary? Because humanity tends toward excess—a tendency that will never end. I do not think I need to explain this. If a person makes excess his goal, it is a bottomless well. We think that if we just had that one more thing, or owned something particular, then we would be happy. At some point, we acquire this thing—say a car or a video—we purchase it, and as it turns out, it is not enough; it is not happiness. Then we need something else, and something else, and so it goes on forever. Hence the most important thing in life is that which is necessary. A person who is free from greed will always feel lighter.

Another important principle comes in the next phrase of the Lord's Prayer: "Forgive us our debts as we forgive our debtors." If we ask God for understanding and for the forgiveness of our wretched souls, and if we believe that He sees us and sees our prayers to the very depths, then should we not also relate to others with similar understanding and forgiveness?

"Lead us not into temptation." I knew a person who strove for a very long time to perform a heroic act, but his friend stopped him. This was during the years of "stagnation,"[20] and it reminded me of the old adage, "Self-inflicted martyrdom receives no crown." During an exam at the Theological Academy, a teacher asked me, "Why do you think the Apostle Peter denied Christ?" I began to suggest different hypotheses, but the teacher said that the main reason was that Peter first announced, "I will follow you to the death, and to prison, and everywhere." Peter was sure of himself. He was willing to put himself in temptation's way, but he failed. A person should not try to tempt fate or to test the Lord God.

Jesus Christ left us this simple but clear prayer, the Lord's Prayer. He also told us, "But you, when you pray, go into your room, and when you have shut your door, pray to your Father who is in the secret place" (Matt. 6:6). At this point, my Baptist friend was right; this is where you need to say all that is on your heart, in your own words. When friends have gathered to pray together, they can pray in their own words as well. But this does not mean that Jesus Christ has rejected sacred forms of recited prayer.

I remind you of one important and tragic moment in Jesus's life. When He was dying on the cross, why did the soldiers say that He called out to Elijah? It was because He prayed using words from a psalm. "'*Eli, Eli, lama sabachthani?*' that is, 'My God, My God, why have You forsaken Me?'" (Matt. 27:46). These are not Christ's words, as some mistakenly think, but they are the beginning of a prayer, the beginning of a biblical psalm that begins with the cry of a suffering man and ends with the triumph of God's help (Ps. 22). In ancient Hebrew, the name Elijah sounds like Iliya; since the word *Eli* was spoken from the distance of the cross, the soldiers may have confused it with the name of Elijah. Thus, Christ used the words of a prayer while He was dying. As the Gospel of Luke recounts, with His last breath He said, "Into Your hands I commit My spirit" (Lk. 23:46). These are words from a prayer the people of the Old Testament spoke as they went to sleep (Ps. 31:5). Jesus had been saying this prayer from childhood. It has also been preserved in the Western liturgy and in many Christian traditions as an evening prayer before bed. "Into Your hands I commit my spirit." This fact alone should show us that formulas are not unimportant.

Another example is of the famous doctor and Nobel Prize winner Alexis Carrel, who became a Christian later in life and witnessed a miraculous healing that took place right before his eyes. I read his description of the event. Carrel is well known in the field of medicine, but he also had a small booklet on prayer printed several years ago in Belgium. As a doctor, he wrote the following: "If you are reading holy words from a prayer book and your thoughts wander off, these words are not spoken in vain."[21]

The first time some of you were in an Orthodox church, you were likely surprised that there are a few short prayers that are repeated many times. "Lord, have mercy" is repeated forty times in a row. The very same requests are made several times. Why is this so? Only part of these prayers make it into our consciousness; the rest falls into our subconscious, into the depths of our being ("Ya"), which is hidden from external influences. Yet we need these very depths shaken up, because they are the source of both sin and goodness.

Not everything that acts on the consciousness influences a person. For this reason, the Orthodox Church has adopted the habit of repeating short prayers. Among these is the Jesus Prayer, which is just a few words in length: "Lord Jesus Christ, Son of God, have mercy on me, a sinner." This prayer is repeated 50 to 100 times using prayer ropes.[22]

The Church Fathers declared the goal of a person's prayerful condition to be unceasing prayer. This may seem strange to you. What kind of person just prays all the time? He must either be crazy, sick, or a fanatic. But in reality, ceaseless prayer is a normal thing and is the goal of the Christian life. This does not mean that a person must always repeat prayers, but it does mean that he is always in God's presence. Whether laughing or crying, tired or energetic, melancholy or joyous, he always sees God in his peripheral vision. This means that he orients himself around God—with thanksgiving, with pleas, with repentance. "Lord, You are right here by my side." Such a state of mind makes a soul steadfast, strong, and enlightened. But in order to reach this point, we must begin with the prayer book.

I have just discussed the highest stages of prayer (see also Chapter Nine). The first steps, however, are morning and evening prayers from the prayer book. It is necessary to read them morning and evening, memorizing them one at a time. It is extraordinarily important to know them by heart, because when you repeat them from memory, they enter into the depths of your soul, and you conquer the surrounding forces of darkness.

Perhaps you are afraid, alarmed, confused, or in a bad mood, but when you begin to pronounce holy words, they begin slowly to bring order to your soul, like Orpheus who could tame wild animals.[23] If it does not help to say these words to yourself, say them aloud. This has been tested, and experience shows that it works.

Prayer gives a person deep strength, because it joins him to God. An example of contemplative prayer comes from Jean-Baptiste-Marie Vianney, a nineteenth-century French Catholic priest. He told a story about how he, when leaving church after Mass, often noticed a peasant who stayed behind and sat there for a long time. In France, the altar was open; on the altar stood the tabernacle where the Holy Gifts were always kept—this was the location of their sanctuary.[24] This person would sit motionlessly and look at that spot. Finally, the priest asked him, "What are you doing here? What are you experiencing?" And the man answered, "I am a simple man and do not know how to tell you, Father. I sit here before Christ, and I am happy here with Him, and probably He with me."[25]

The apostles experienced this feeling of God's presence at the mystery of the Transfiguration while they slept on the mountain. When the three apostles awakened to see Christ shining, they did not know what to say. Peter said, "It is good for us to be here" (Mk. 9:5). This is the height of an inner prayerful presence.

Metropolitan Anthony (Bloom), one of our modern theologians and teachers of prayer, told the story of one woman who could not feel the power of prayer, no matter what she did. She said, "God is silent when I pray." The metropolitan responded, "Well, ma'am, you do not give Him a chance to get a word in edgewise. Something in your mind is making noise. How can you hear His soft voice if you are always telling Him something?"[26] Of course, the metropolitan always spoke and wrote about this with a tinge of irony, but this story has a profound meaning: we do not know how to remain in inner silence for even a few seconds, and therefore the depths of life are not revealed to us. Yet, it is only in these depths that we meet God and find strength, the source of happiness, and the fullness and beauty of life. So, besides reading from the prayer book, we need to learn how to be alone for a few minutes. I say "minutes," because we are all busy people. We all are hurrying somewhere. We all have our own tasks and obligations. Nonetheless, we must set aside these minutes.

And when others of you say that this is impossible, there is a clear and simple answer. No matter what kind of hurry a person is in, he must eat and drink. Sometimes in a flurry of work, he may forget about food and drink. But would he last very long? No, he would still need to strengthen himself. Doesn't the soul also need nourishment? We just do not feel the soul's sufferings as clearly as the sufferings of the stomach, but the consequences of neglecting the soul's needs may be even more lethal.

For this reason, the Church has instituted a rule, almost a law, that we begin and end each day with the prayer book. If praying from the prayer book stirs up a prayerful inner state, then this is a victory, happiness, and success. Things have worked out well. And if not? It is still better than if you had begun your day by simply washing, heating breakfast, running from here to there and going to work befuddled.

We must also consider practical life issues. Some people come home after work so exhausted they cannot read evening prayers. There is a solution to this: we can always find seven minutes some time before bed. This is in our best interest, and it must become a habit. I will say, taking full responsibility, that if you institute this practice in your life, it will begin to bring results within one month. As soon as you start to pray "according to your mood"—today I want to, tomorrow I do not—your spiritual state will decline. A person who performs any task, be it creative, musical, artistic, or athletic, must be "in shape." If it has been a long time since he has played, picked up his instrument, or done any exercise, he will fall out of shape. In the same way, our soul gets out of shape if it does not perform elementary spiritual exercises such as prayer or meditating on the Holy Scriptures.

Meditation on the Holy Scriptures is important for the individual, spiritual being. These days, nearly all of you have the Gospels, or even the whole Bible.[27] Do not think, however, that you have to read it in large chunks, but rather a little at a time, systematically, every day. Then, it will begin to enter into you. And if within one month you memorize just one biblical verse or passage, know that you have taken a huge step, because it will stay with you forever. You will not need to haphazardly flip pages. It will be with you and will come to you as the living Word of God the very moment it is needed, as encouragement, warning, or direction.

This meditation on God's Word opens up special worlds. When you leave for work in the morning, you take this Word with you; it is present with you, and you ponder it. Just as a vine weaves itself around the trunk of a tree, your soul weaves itself around this truth. You may be riding the subway in a crowd of rude, pushy, and unpleasant people, but you are protected. You go on, protected by a spiritual wall. You begin to build what Antoine de Saint-Exupery called an inner citadel.[28]

This does not mean that you become thick-skinned and indifferent, but you are strengthened. Your reactions stop being so explosive. You are not as easily wounded or as vulnerable as you had been previously, because you are with Him and you see the world through this prism. And immediately a new dimension and a new depth are opened up, and you perceive the people you see in a new way. You now experience goodwill, compassion, humanity—almost love—toward these people. And it is no longer unpleasant for you to ride on the escalator and see people's depressed expressions. You see them differently now. Everyday life—the simple, common stuff—begins to change. You stop being an unhappy person who is disgusted by everything, who is nauseated when glancing around, who feels as if you have been submerged into some kind of mud. Of course, life is not sugar, but when and where has it ever been sugar? The important thing is that a person strengthened by God would know how to preserve and develop himself in this life. Therefore, meditating on the Holy Scriptures and using the prayer book are part of the Christian life. I like to call them two "stool legs."[29]

A third "stool leg" is Sunday. I have always been pleased when foreign hockey teams come to the Soviet Union and say, "We do not play on Sundays." Is this formalism or ritualism? No, it is faithfulness to an ancient principle. Over three thousand years ago, the Lord said, "Keep the Sabbath" (Ex. 31:14),[30] and this is now a habit for us. We have one or two days of rest per week. Actually, this day was given from the beginning so humanity could get out of the never-ending rat race,[31] stop to think, and come to its senses. You all know very well that you will never get all the work done; it is a bottomless barrel. It is worth it to stop and gain the strength needed for life. Only then will our work go better.

There is a story about a German shoemaker whose pastor repeatedly asked him to go to church. He would answer, "Of course, I honor the Lord our God, but I have a family and must make shoes on Sunday as well, in order to feed them." Then the pastor did an experiment. He said, "How much do you make on Sundays? I'll pay you that much for three months, so you can come to church." They agreed. As a result, the shoemaker was able to make up for the lost day, and Sunday became for him a source of celebrating life.

What is life without celebration? Nothing but gray slush.[32] Thus, Sunday should be a celebration for us. We have lost and neglected this principle. Today, we only recall this from literature and not from our fathers' and grandfathers' stories.[33] We need to remember that on Sunday they used to even dress for a celebration. They loved Sunday—pies and more! Today this sounds crazy; everything has been mixed together. Sunday is now a day for doing laundry and such. So the third element—the third stool leg—is the holy day of Resurrection (Sunday).[34]

Of course, at the center of all this is our communal prayer. You may ask, "How can we talk to God all together?" Yes, Christ said, "Pray alone"; but He also said, "Where two or three are gathered together in My name, I am there in the midst of them" (Matt. 18:20). This means that we surrender our hearts to Him and serve Him together. And this constitutes true service to God, in worship.

PART TWO

A PRACTICAL GUIDE TO PRAYER

This section constitutes a small instructional book that Father Alexander wrote and shared with his parishioners. He initially designed it to be used within clandestine "small groups" in the late 1970s and early 1980s. His church's small groups focused on various themes. The ones that focused specifically on studying and practicing prayer utilized this work in manuscript form.

CHAPTER THREE

INTRODUCTION

F AITH, A LIVING CONNECTION BETWEEN OUR SOUL AND GOD, is not something immutable; it is not inherited in its final form. As with any relationship, faith has its own dynamic; it can become weak, or conversely, it can strengthen and grow. The formation of faith within a person is connected with the will, mind, and emotions. The increase of faith is inseparable from the three main ways of drawing near to God: (1) moral efforts directed toward good, (2) the battle with one's inner enemy (also known as *askesis*), and (3) prayer, to which the following pages are dedicated.

Saint Mark the Ascetic says, "Let us begin the work of prayer and, gradually making progress, we shall find that not only hope in God but also firm faith and unfeigned love, absence of rancor, love for one's brethren, self-mastery, patience, the innermost knowledge, deliverance from temptations, gifts of grace, heartfelt profession of faith, and fervent tears are given to the faithful through prayer."[35] From this saint's words, it is clear how greatly significant prayer is for the Christian and how many facets of life are affected by it. Prayer binds our spirit to the very Source of Life. Neither theological theories nor good deeds can replace prayer. Both of these things are given life through prayer, which keeps our faith from straying into distraction or moralizing.

For an inexperienced person, the old adage "prayer is hard work" may sound strange, but those who have taken even their first few spiritual steps know how many obstacles must be overcome before they attain the gift of prayer. God is accessible to everyone, but all too often the rays of His grace fall on the deaf ears and locked doors of our souls. How can we open them? How can we prepare ourselves to meet the Ineffable One?

Saints and ascetics, people with rich spiritual experience, have spoken about this. They have considered it necessary to share with others what they have learned on the path of prayer. However, what they have left behind is too extensive, and so often the writings of ascetics are connected to life conditions that are far removed from how we live now. The goal of this book is to highlight the parts of these writings that give concrete guidance to the modern person.

This "guide" is meant for those who have already passed through the beginning stages of the Christian life and desire to deepen it. As a guide, it assumes that the reader is *familiar with the Holy Scriptures and the fundamentals of the Church's teachings*. It also assumes that the reader regularly *participates in church services and sacraments*.

There are numerous excellent books about prayer written for our contemporaries, including the works of Metropolitan Anthony (Bloom) of Sourozh.[36] In the next several chapters, however, we will focus primarily on the practical side of the life of prayer—what aids it and what hinders it. Therefore, you should not look upon this guide as "a book to be read." It requires slow, attentive study as well as the practical application of the advice offered. For this reason, it is written in a condensed, outlined, and schematic fashion—a method that best facilitates assimilation and true learning. This guide is organized with a dual structure. The chapters are placed in order of difficulty. They are also designed in such a way that the reader can regularly refer to what has already been read, since many topics are parallel to each other.

I essentially say nothing from myself. Nearly the entire text consists of the works of the Church Fathers, ascetics, and spiritual writers of the East and West. Of those from the West, you will mostly encounter the works of a modern teacher of prayer, the priest-monk Father Henri Caffarel.[37] I extend heartfelt thanks to all who have made this book possible.

May God strengthen all who embark on the difficult but blessed path of prayer.

CHAPTER FOUR

PRAYER AND THE PRAYER BOOK

E VERY PERSON HAS MOMENTS WHEN HIS SOUL INVOLUNTARILY surges upward in a burst of prayer—tragic turning points in life; the awe of a soul overtaken by creative inspiration or touched by beauty. These moments can awaken the power that lifts us up to God in supplication, thanksgiving, and joy. But here, I will speak mainly about *systematic* prayer, which enters into life as a constant companion and inspirer.

THE PRAYER BOOK

The prayer book is an initial and necessary form of prayer. This is called the reading of a "prayer rule," which consists of morning and evening prayers spoken every day. This rhythm is necessary, lest the soul fall away from the life of prayer, awakening only as circumstance prompts. In prayer, just as in every great and difficult task, it is insufficient to rely solely on flashes of inspiration, the right mood, or improvisation.

There are three main kinds of prayer rules:[38]

1. A *complete prayer rule* is designed for people who have more time than others. It can be found in prayer books used by hierarchs and clergy.

2. A *short rule* is designed for everyone. Morning and evening prayers can be found in any prayer book.

3. A *minimal rule:* The prayer rule of Saint Seraphim of Sarov, for example, consists of reciting "Our Father" (the

Lord's Prayer) three times, "Rejoice, O Virgin" three times (see Appendix D), and the Nicene Creed once. Such a prayer rule is for those days and circumstances when a person finds herself in extreme fatigue or does not have sufficient time for the other rules.

It is dangerous to completely skip the prayer rule. Exhaustion and distraction should not prevent us from reading it (see Chapter Six). Even if the rule is not read with the necessary level of attention, the words of the prayers work their way into the subconscious and exert their sanctifying work. A person looking at a picture or icon, or listening to music or poetry, is joined to the inner world of its maker. In a similar way, the reading of prayers connects us to their creators— the psalmists and ascetics. It helps us to acquire a spiritual attitude akin to the fire in their hearts. Father Alexander Elchaninov writes, "[A]n example is offered us by Christ. His prayer and lamentations on the Cross are 'quotations' from the psalms" (Ps. 22:1, 31:5).[39]

PREPARING FOR THE PRAYER RULE

It is good to *memorize* the main prayers, so they can penetrate deeper into our hearts and can be repeated in any situation. Nicodemus of the Holy Mountain advises, "Try to ponder over and feel the prayers you have to read, not at the hour of prayer, but at some other free time. If you do this, then, at the time set for prayer, you will have no difficulty in reproducing in yourself the whole content of the prayer you read."[40]

When beginning your prayer rule, it is critical to dispel all resentment, frustration, and bitterness. Tikhon of Zadonsk says, "Before prayer, it is necessary neither to be angry with anyone nor to be wrathful, but to forgive all who have offended us, so that God would forgive our sins."[41]

Without effort directed toward the battle against sin, toward serving people, and toward gaining control over the body and the spiritual life, prayer cannot be what it is meant to be—an inner support for our lives (see Chapter Five on asceticism). Reading, especially the reading of the Gospels, plays an important role in training a prayerful spirit, as do the sacraments of Confession and the Eucharist (see Appendix B).

Communion of the Holy Mysteries (i.e., taking Communion) draws the whole person into the sacred stream of a life of grace. It is harmful to take Communion infrequently, because this estranges us from the help of grace. In the past, the practice arose of rarely taking Communion—a practice condemned by the Holy Fathers. Bishop Theophan the Recluse wrote, "Here in Russia, people are even saying that it is a sin to take Communion often; others comment that it is forbidden to take Communion more frequently than every six weeks. Perhaps there are others besides these who share this same wrong attitude. Do not listen to such talk. Take Communion as often as necessary, without hesitation. But do make every effort to prepare yourself fully as prescribed by the Church, and come with fear and trembling, with faith, contrition, and repentance. If anyone interferes, reply, 'I come to Holy Communion each time with the permission of my spiritual father.'"[42]

TIME AND PLACE

In the modern world, with its demands and quick pace, it is not easy to set aside a specific time for prayer. Nonetheless, it is best to read morning prayers before beginning anything. In extreme cases, you could say them on your commute to work. Late at night, it is often difficult to concentrate due to fatigue; thus, teachers of prayer recommend reading evening prayers in the free moments before dinner or even earlier.

If possible, it is good to be alone or to stand before an icon while praying. There is no simple answer to the question of whether the whole family or each person individually should read the prayer rule. The answer depends upon a person's character and upon a family's relationships. Communal prayer is recommended primarily on important occasions such as a holiday feast. Family prayer is a kind of ecclesiastical prayer ("the home church") and should, therefore, not replace individual prayer, but may supplement it.

BEGINNING TO PRAY

Before reading prayers, we make the sign of the cross and, having cast aside all our everyday cares, we try to focus on our inner conversation with God. The Russian prayer book provides the following instruction: "Stand silently until all emotions are calm. Place yourself in God's presence, until you are conscious of Him and can feel Him with reverent fear. In your heart, raise up a banner of living faith that God hears and sees you."

DURING PRAYER

Beginners should read the prayers aloud or in a soft voice. This helps with concentration.

If your own prayers come spilling out while reading the prayer rule, then, as Saint Nicodemus says, "Do not let this occasion slip by, but pause and pray in your own words."[43] Bishop Theophan expresses the same idea: "When you experience a strong feeling of prayer interrupting your prayer rule, stop reading and give space to this feeling."[44]

Many people think prayer should always bring "spiritual pleasure." They forget about the difficult character of prayer. "Do not search for delights in prayer," says Bishop Ignatius Brianchaninov, "for they are far from inherent to a sinner. A sinner's desire to experience delight is already a form of self-deceit. Do not prematurely seek a high spiritual state or prayerful ecstasy."[45] Notice that the search for constant spiritual enjoyment is a hidden form of selfishness and a pursuit of spiritual comfort. The difficulty of prayer is often a sign of its authenticity (see Chapter Six).

Praying for others is an indispensable part of the prayer rule. To stand before God does not draw us away from others, but rather binds us to them with even tighter bonds. The poet Alexei K. Tolstoy describes this very well:

> To ask God in faith that He would remove misfortune from a loved one is not a fruitless work, as is supposed by some philosophers who acknowledge prayer only as a way to worship God, to fellowship with Him, and to feel His presence. First and foremost, prayer has a direct and powerful influence on the soul of the person for whom you are praying. The closer you are to God, the more you become independent from your body. Thus, *your soul is less limited* by the space and material that separates you from the soul for whom you are praying. I am nearly convinced that two people praying simultaneously for each other with the same fervent faith could commune with one another without any material aids, despite their physical separation. How can we know the extent to which the circumstances of a loved one have been predestined? And if these circumstances have been subjected to an array of influences, what could have a stronger influence than a soul drawing near to God with a burning desire that all circumstances would come together for the good of a friend's soul?[46]

We should not limit ourselves to praying only for our friends and loved ones, however. Prayer for those who have grieved us also brings peace to our souls and has an influence on these people. And our prayer becomes sacrificial.

THE END OF THE PRAYER RULE

It is good to end the prayer rule with thanksgiving to God for the gift of fellowship, and with contrition for our lack of attention. Saint Nicodemus teaches, "Do not at once throw yourself into daily affairs and never think that, having performed your rule of prayer, you have finished with your duty to God and can now give rein to your thoughts and feelings."[47]

As we begin our tasks, we need to think about what stands before us to say, do, and see throughout the day. We need to ask God for a blessing and for the strength to follow His will. Sometimes it is good in the thick of the workday to have one word or a short prayer that would help us to find the Lord in everyday tasks (see Chapter Seven). We must also approach God in our thoughts before the start of each task and before meals.

Now that we have discussed the process of praying with a prayer book, let us proceed to the next chapter, where we will discuss the significance of our bodies in prayer.

CHAPTER FIVE

THE BODY AND PRAYER *(Askesis)*

S IS TRUE FOR THE SPIRITUAL LIFE IN GENERAL, PRAYER should not remain an isolated corner of our existence. Humanity is called to be whole and harmonious. Thus, we must keep in mind all spheres of our being when discussing the act of prayer. A correct understanding of one's design is necessary. Bishop Theophan writes, "Once we have established reasonable concepts about man's make-up, we will have the most reliable indication as to how he is to live."[48] Following a widely accepted tradition, Bishop Theophan divides the human being into three basic spheres: body, soul, and spirit. Body and soul (psyche) constitute what the Bible calls "the flesh."

The spirit is the part of the person made in the likeness of God, the focal point of the person where self-awareness, will, freedom, creativity, and conscience are made manifest. By its very nature, the spirit is designed to rule over the flesh. The spirit is the highest part within the human being, distinguishing him from all creation. This does not mean, however, that the psychophysical level is just an unnecessary and burdensome vessel. It is tightly connected to the spirit. As the simplest emotions can grow into elevated experiences that ascend into the spiritual sphere, so elements of thought (characteristic even of animals) can rise to the spiritual level, joining the "lower mind" with the "higher mind." The area of thought influences our emotions, and vice versa. Emotions are tightly woven together with the life of the body. It could be said that in mankind (a "microcosm," or little world), the whole of nature enters into a deep unity with the kingdom of the spirit. This location on the boundary between the natural and spiritual worlds makes mankind the embodiment of the universe, the entity through which natural existence ascends to God. Therefore, when we build a spiritual life within ourselves, we must consider our hierarchical structure and strive to include our *entire* being in our walk with God.

Metropolitan Anthony writes, "The body participates (noticeably or not) in every movement of the soul, be it a feeling, an abstract thought, a desire, or a supersensory experience."[49] Consequently, the body plays a critical role in prayer. Those who forget this will inevitably run into many difficulties. We must give up our pagan view of the flesh as deserving nothing more than contempt, or as the "prison of the soul." The human body is God's wondrous creation, the most perfect creation in all of nature. A person is not simply "imprisoned" within his body, but lives by it, expressing all of his aspirations through it. The mystery of the Incarnation is a great testimony against those who would view the body from the point of view of non-Christian dualism and spiritualism. These views are remnants of ancient Eastern beliefs and the teachings of Plato, but they are by no means attributable to the Bible or Christianity.

It would be just as false, however, to put the body in an undeserving position, submitting to its every demand. Our *entire* existence, which carries the stamp of original sin on it, is marked by a dissonance between the spirit and the flesh. Therefore, many natural instincts stand in opposition to the spiritual life. This is why the New Testament and the Church Fathers warn against following the flesh; remember that by "the flesh," the Scriptures mean mankind's whole psychophysical nature. Saint Basil the Great compares the body with a horse that requires a bit. Just as an uncontrollable horse will throw its rider, so the flesh, if left to its own devices, will enslave the spirit. Conversely, the body, when put in its proper place, is capable of *assisting* the spiritual life and prayer (something altogether different from simply *not impeding* prayer). Both the neglect and the undue elevation of the body can seriously backfire and destroy the life of the soul and spirit. The art of controlling the body and managing the flesh is called asceticism (see the *Askesis* section below).

Healthy or ailing, rejoicing or suffering, our body must be the vessel of our soul, the instrument of its expression while striving for the higher life. This is why the Apostle Paul calls the body "the temple of the Holy Spirit" (1 Cor. 6:19). The Church, therefore, reverently venerates saints' relics. As the Apostle Paul commands, we are to honor God with our bodies (1 Cor. 6:20).

BODY POSITIONS AND PRAYERFUL GESTURES

Abba Isaiah says, "When you are in your cell and stand to say your prayers, do not be careless in negligence.[50] Do not lean against the wall or give in to your legs, standing on one and lifting the other as fools do."[51] He said this with a purpose. There are certain psychophysical mechanisms that create a connection between the position of the body and the state of the soul and spirit. It is difficult to pray while sprawled out in a recliner, for example. Certain body positions and gestures better facilitate prayer and promote inner concentration. The first among these gestures is *the sign of the cross*—the cross of Christ traced on our bodies. From ancient times, bowing (either from the waist or full prostrations) has been given much meaning. These body positions contribute to the strengthening of feelings of reverence, humility, and worship.

Prayer while standing is the standard body position while praying. It is an expression of alertness, composure, and readiness to attend.

1. While standing during prayer, one must strive for balance, stability, and a relaxed pose. Let's examine the position of different parts of the body. The *soles of your feet* should be flat on the floor and next to each other (or spread a bit apart). Do not tense the *upper part of your legs*. The proper position of the *back* is also necessary for balance and stability; the *torso* should be straight but not tense, allowing for natural curvature. The *shoulders* should be down and relaxed. You should not keep your *head* bowed or raised for long periods.

2. The position of your *hands* is also quite important. They can be used as an external expression of our internal condition. In recent centuries in the Orthodox Church, it has become tradition that only the priest raises his hands during the church service. However, this ancient gesture can be used in private prayer. The Scriptures mention this regularly (see Lam. 3:41 and 1 Tim. 2:8).

3. Your *eyes* should not wander. It is necessary to focus them on an icon or to close them. Otherwise, concentration is easily broken.

Prayer while on your knees expresses repentance, humility, and supplication. It is difficult, however, to keep this position stable for very long.

Prayer while sitting is not recommended during the prayer rule (exceptions may be made for the sick and fatigued). This is, however, a perfectly good position for prayerful meditation and deep prayers (see Chapter Seven). In this position, one needs to pay attention to the natural straightness of the body and the natural position of the head. Otherwise, the body could fall asleep and you might get light-headed.

While using any body position, you must make sure that (1) the position is held correctly, (2) there is no tension in the muscles or nerves, (3) you are breathing properly, and (4) you are maintaining inner silence. At the beginning, most of these positions require constant practice that is always flexible and never excessive. The positions do not need to be kept for long periods of time. It is a sign that the position is correct and well chosen if you feel comfortable, stable, and unconstrained. If a position is uncomfortable after you try it a few times, abstain from using it. Metropolitan Philaret says, "It is better to sit and think about God than to stand and think about your feet."[52] A body position should coincide with one or another inner condition expressed by that position. At the same time, an inner condition supports and gives life to a body position.

You should never abruptly change positions. First, you can rub your hands, open and close your eyes, wiggle your feet, or straighten your knees. Then, assume a transitional position. For example, if your body is prostrated on the ground, you should get up on your knees before standing.

BREATHING

Orthodox ascetics often talk about the connection between breathing and prayer.[53] When a natural and healthy dynamic is achieved, breathing gradually calms the body, pacifies the senses, and strengthens the mind. In so doing, it prepares the whole person for prayer.

There are special exercises designed to regulate breathing (see Appendix A). If you do not have the opportunity to perform all of these exercises, it is good to inhale and exhale deeply two or three times before beginning to pray. Then, having allowed your breathing to return to its normal rhythm, you need not focus on it the rest of the time.

ASKESIS

Asceticism (from the Greek word *askesis*, or *exercise*) is the effort we must exert in order to open ourselves to the influence of God's Spirit. Asceticism is vital and should encompass *our entire life*, so that grace can turn our every action toward God. Thus, asceticism is lived out in our basic tasks—in relaxation, in our diet, and in our relationships.

Selfishness and a tendency toward foolishness reside in each of us. It is necessary to put selfishness to death, crowding it out with love, and to attempt to control the spontaneous whims of the flesh. Asceticism assumes systematic and well-considered actions. All the same, it is necessary to avoid any extremism and to be very careful. Brute force could lead to destruction in the life of the body, the soul, and, consequently, the spirit. The criterion used to evaluate the effectiveness of our asceticism should be *our attitude toward others*. If it does not change for the better, then no spiritual feat will have any worth, and we run the risk of falling into false mysticism and self-delusion.

In no way is asceticism the suppression of human nature, but rather it is a way to introduce our nature to a genuinely healthy rhythm. The chaos of thoughts, feelings, and desires is an anomaly. Asceticism fights against this anomaly.

Fasting

From the most ancient times, it has been observed that animal (meat) products have a noticeably undesirable effect on people. Therefore, Eastern religions developed the principle of vegetarianism. The Bible, conceding to human weakness, does not forbid animal products as food (Gen. 9:3). The Church does limit its consumption, however, by imposing extended and one-day fasts (see Appendix B).[54]

There are three goals of fasting: (1) a temporary separation from animal products, (2) an exercise of the will through obedience to the

Church, and (3) a connection of the daily meal with the liturgical year. Undoubtedly, there are circumstances that require a lessening or a suspension of a fast (e.g., traveling, illness, protests by family members, or other special life situations). In these cases, abstinence from food can be substituted with any other form of abstinence. We must avoid two extremes: making the fast into something absolute and incontestable, or neglecting the fast altogether.

Abstaining from food can be detrimental to the soul if a person turns the fast into a cult practice and is filled with thoughts of superiority. Saint Mark the Ascetic says, "Fasting is beneficial for those who approach it wisely but harmful to those who begin to fast unwisely. Those wishing to gain from the fast, therefore, must beware of its danger, namely vainglory."[55] Saints Barsanuphius and John say, "If anyone, while keeping a fast, adds something to it by his own will, or if he fasts seeking men's praise or some gain from it, such a fast is an abomination in God's eyes."[56]

A fast consists not only of abstinence from food, but also of a temporary intensification of the battle against the passions. Metropolitan Anthony asserts, "A fast is first and foremost a movement, an activity of the Spirit, and a battle against stagnation, laziness, over-sensitivity, and weakness of will and body. This is a fight for life and for the liberation of the spirit from its accustomed slavery."[57]

Bodily asceticism includes general life discipline and concern for a balanced lifestyle (work and play), proper sleep (avoiding late night conversations, etc.), and taking care of the nervous system (not abusing stimulants or tonics). Ascetic limitations, in part, help to establish control over the chaotic desires of the body. We must train ourselves for physical labor and for some physical chastisement: excessive comforts in no way aid the spiritual life.

Working on the Areas of Emotion, Desire, and Thought

Emotions, desires, and thoughts are closely connected to the body. Therefore, it is necessary to take care of these "eyes of the soul," particularly by making a "covenant with my eyes," as Job did (Job 31:1).

There is a difference between foolish desires (which should not be satisfied at all) and natural desires (which should simply be limited, so we can learn to control them or to keep them within their proper bounds). Throughout the day there are a thousand opportunities to train yourself in the direction of your spiritual aspirations. For example, you could come to the assistance of a neighbor, stop reading emotionally charged literature,[58] accept criticism gracefully, or learn to listen.

The battle against evil thoughts that inevitably come into the consciousness should move in two directions:

1. Constant training to attain mental control (see Appendix A) and

2. Calm rejection of these thoughts as something foreign and tainted by dark forces. Saint Theodoros the Great Ascetic says, "He who is battling to repulse what harasses and wars against him must enlist the help of other allies—I mean humility of soul, bodily toil and every other kind of ascetic hardship, together with prayer that springs from an afflicted heart and is accompanied by many tears."[59]

It is not good to cultivate any desire that might rule over the mind. It is essential to avoid daydreaming and to train the mind to return to thoughts about God—"to bring the mind to the heart," as ascetics suggest. This phrase signifies victory over the division of the human being and the restoration of *wholeness*, when both the mind and the senses are directed toward *a single Center*—God. According to Symeon the New Theologian, the true image "of attention and prayer . . . is as follows: the mind, while praying, . . . guards the heart. It remains in the heart and from those depths, it sends prayers to God."[60] Your "You" ("*Ya*") must live wholly in the present moment, fully joining with God's will. It is necessary to try to complete the task at hand as well as possible, sweeping aside cares about the past and the future.

A Deceptive Orientation of the Spirit

A person should aim to control himself with all his might—not for the sake of a prideful feeling of power over self, but in order to submit to God's will. The human spirit can also be deceptively oriented. The pursuit of the absolute, the wonderful, and the just can be egotistical. We should check and, when necessary, correct our motivations.

The highest goal of Christianity is always God, who is sought *selflessly*. With every prayer, one must consciously direct one's whole self and life toward God. At some point, according to Starets Silouan, a "yearning for God" awakens in the spirit.[61] But even with this, the temptation of selfishness can infiltrate the heart (e.g., the urge to leave everyone and immerse oneself in one's own inner world). We must remind ourselves that *serving others* is *serving Christ* (see Matt. 25:40). This service, however, must be augmented with deep soul-searching. We must be able to constantly return to our own spirit, the abode of the Spirit of God. We do this in order to acquire fresh bursts of faith, hope, and love, which will strengthen our bond with God in anticipation of the day when unceasing prayer will well up inside us.

CHAPTER SIX
DIFFICULTIES IN PRAYER

T HERE IS NO REASON TO FALL INTO DESPAIR AND MISERY from
the abundance of hindrances encountered while praying.
They are inevitable and may in some ways be helpful for
the soul. Starets Macarius of Optina taught that "prayer without
diversion (distraction) is achieved by the mature. . . . But if they
[the mature] always had pure prayer without distraction, then they
would not be able to avoid the vainglorious and proud thoughts
sent by the enemy."[62] Nonetheless, the same starets teaches on the
importance of an unrelenting battle with temptations that disturb
prayer. Let's discuss some of the difficulties experienced during
prayer.

DISTRACTION

Distraction is the main obstacle to prayer. People often believe
that everyday tasks are the main cause of distraction, but this is only
partly true. Bishop Theophan the Recluse says that distraction comes
"not from the nature of our everyday responsibilities, but from our
carelessness, by which we allow ourselves to immerse our thoughts,
feelings, desires, and cares only in worldly things. But surely it does
not have to be this way. Begin everything with prayer, continue with
hope, and end with thanksgiving."[63]

Many forms of distraction reveal the undesirable orientation and
enslavement of our soul. We must uncover the source of our hidden
ambitions and then either lead them in the right direction or take

control of them. If distraction does not go away, we must learn to treat it as a temptation—patiently and without irritation. As long as distractions have not overtaken our very soul ("*Ya*") (i.e., as long as our soul ("*Ya*") is consciously turned toward God and not to the thing distracting us), prayer still lingers. If we *suffer* because outside thoughts appear, it is a sure sign that our soul ("*Ya*") is not defeated and that it continues to resist distraction.

How can we resist outside thoughts? If these thoughts are lustful or blasphemous, then we must remind ourselves that they are demonic temptations invading our inner world. In other cases, we must realize that sinful thoughts are, at their core, internal manifestations of various aspects of our being. We must fight their uncontrolled expression. This may mean we need to rein in gluttony, laziness, carnality, or excessive flights of imagination. We must strengthen our spirit by directing it toward God.

We should actively resist distractions and include all dimensions of our being in prayer (directing our gaze on an icon, our imagination on biblical events, and our thoughts on spiritual things, which in turn will strengthen love and reverence within us). If our prayer is disrupted by serious anxiety about something or someone, then let this anxiety be included in that prayer, so that the problem would become a factor that helps to strengthen the prayer for those people and situations that are causing us such concern.

A DRY HEART

Dryness of heart is felt especially acutely in contrast to moments of grace. Physical or nervous exhaustion can intensify this feeling. In this case, it is necessary to exercise care in removing (or decreasing) the causes of this dryness of heart.[64] Dryness may be the result of any type of sin or mistake. In such cases, it is necessary to call attention to the sin and sincerely repent and to approach dryness as a deserved trial. It is often impossible to pinpoint the sin that is causing dryness. At such times, having given a general confession, we must wait patiently for this condition to pass.

Saint Francis de Sales said, "At first, God gives spiritual joy in order to draw a person away from worldly pleasures and to prompt him to strive for spiritual love. . . . Sometimes God later removes these comforts to teach us a more steadfast reverence in the midst of trials and temptations."[65] In this way, dryness could be given to us as an exercise in patience unto perfection. And actually, thanks to dryness, our faith is purified. "Blessed are those who have not seen and yet have believed" (John 20:29). Love is also purified, for we must seek God Himself, and not the joy that comes from Him. And hope is strengthened—hope for God's return to a soul that is weary from dryness.

Thus, whatever the reason for our dryness and barrenness of spirit, this difficult condition may in the end indirectly help us to move along the spiritual path. In such cases, there is no need to despair or to strain. We must preserve peace, remembering that the Lord will not leave us, even in periods of numbness and weakness.

SPIRITUAL TENSION

> *Father Alexander uses the term* napriazhenie *throughout this section. This term can be translated as "stress," "straining or striving," "exertion," or "tension." For consistency, we have chosen to utilize the term* tension/tense. *Father Alexander is identifying the particular difficulty of being reliant upon our own effort to acquire spiritual benefits through prayer, rather than allowing God to work in us. In Appendix A, he recommends ways to combat* napriazhenie.

If we are constantly tense, this will be reflected in our prayer. It even happens that some people who are not tense in life are tense in prayer. Tension disrupts prayer, but peace facilitates it. As with every other activity, prayer proceeds against the backdrop of various types of stressors: physical, emotional, and mental. These are often the reason for our distraction. In all actuality, the energy exerted by this tension seeks to capture the mind and divert our attention away from God.

For some people, prayer is associated with unhealthy excitement and spiritual tension—both of which directly contradict prayer. Such tension inadvertently sweeps a person into a state that is harmful for the spiritual life. We can do nothing without grace. *Prayer is much more God's action upon us, than it is our own personal efforts.* Spiritual tension incites us to seek only flashes of inspiration, to desire tangible expressions of grace and the attainment of certain emotional states. In the process, we forget that God is the root of our prayer.

A state of silence and peace is the fundamental condition for prayer. It is necessary to calm oneself before prayer, even if the one praying does not use special techniques to assist in achieving inner silence. Techniques could include listening to appropriate music, slow movements, or a prayerful body position (see Chapter Five). To oppose spiritual tension, you must exclusively pursue God in prayer and deny your own will for His sake, seeking neither understanding nor grace. You must also consecrate your whole life to God, with a spirit of faith and humility.

At the same time, prayer aids in the acquisition of peace and silence in all your being. Of course, *prayer does not exist for the purpose of achieving this peace, but solely for the glory of God.* Nonetheless, the prolonged calm associated with prayer, which causes us to be still and to breathe rhythmically, is the main physical factor contributing to the dissipation of tension. In this way, we see that prayer removes both spiritual and emotional tension. "And the peace of God, which surpasses all understanding, will guard your hearts and minds through Christ Jesus" (Phil. 4:7).

CHAPTER SEVEN

PRAYERFUL MEDITATIONS

THE HOLY SCRIPTURES AND THE CHURCH CALL US TO DEEPEN and to perfect prayer, so that it can draw our spirit closer and closer to God and can sanctify our entire life. We should gradually supplement our reading of the prayer rule with deep prayer, which in turn is the doorway to the highest stages of prayer.

Deep prayer involves turning to God with the full concentration of our inner strength. It is a conversation, a contemplation, or a silent, prayerful pose in His presence. Here the prayer rule is not enough, and the ten to fifteen minutes dedicated to it are insufficient. This type of prayer requires at least half an hour and sometimes an hour every day. Understandably, very few people have such an opportunity, so it is a good idea to start with one or two times a week. Deep prayer grows out of the prayer rule, and prayerful meditation serves as good preparation for deep prayer.

In our everyday lives, there are many moments when we can turn our thoughts toward God (see Chapter Eight). Moments of rest, walks in nature, reading, meetings with people, and even work—all of these provide opportunities for us to contemplate God. We must strive to nurture within ourselves the feeling of the Father's constant presence. Then there will be nothing "worldly" for us, because everything will become holy, and everything will flow into God's realm. Outside of Him, there is only sin; yet even sin, through repentance, can turn us back to Christ.

All that is wonderful and all that brings us joy flows from Him. He gave us our "daily bread," the beauty of the earth, and the joy of our work and human companionship. He gave us our very existence and brought us into this difficult and wonderful life, so we could journey through it discovering and building His Kingdom. One early Christian writer, Hermas, depicted the Church in the form of a tower being built.[66] The souls of the faithful are the stones used to build the tower. This idea should rule in our lives.

What does the Lord expect from us? How can we fulfill His will? A proper understanding of the Christian life depends upon the way we answer these questions. First and foremost, He does not exist for us, but rather we exist for Him. We must surrender and *dedicate* our every step to Him: sadness and joy, knowledge and labor—everything should stand under the banner of prayers of gratitude. In moments of sorrow, even though we know that He knows everything about us, we open our hearts to Him. And no matter what we may ask of Him, our petition should conclude with the statement, "Thy will be done."

An important help in spiritual meditation is *reading*, especially the reading of Scripture. Focused, prayerful reading is performed unhurriedly—reading a bit at a time, pausing to pray to Christ, and asking Him to enlighten our minds. As we pray, it is good to make the sign of the cross or to stand before an icon before returning back to reading. It is important to realize that the words of Scripture are directed to each one of us as a call, a rebuke, or an encouragement. Then, reading imperceptibly becomes a dialogue, a prayerful conversation with God. It would be good if such reading of Scripture and books about the spiritual life could be done every day. If that is not possible, choose three days (Sunday, Wednesday, and Friday) for spiritual reading, or at the very least Sundays and feast days.[67]

The rhythm of human life is associated with a balance between socialization and solitude. By necessity, we spend the greatest part of our life with people, but we must balance this with *minutes of inner silence*. These minutes precede our meditation and prayer. At first, let it be one or two minutes. In this time, we must seek to eliminate all outside thoughts and external and internal hindrances and should choose a place where there are fewer causes for distraction.

In these minutes, we try to "listen" to our body, calm it down, shut off the flow of outside thoughts, and "attend to the silence." After this, we slowly and thoughtfully say to ourselves a prayer of our choice. The best one is the "Our Father" (Lord's Prayer). Each time, we should take just one word or short phrase and pause to reflect upon it. "Our Father." Father—the all-encompassing Bosom of Love, the Creator and Leader. For a while, we consider the fact that at one time we did not exist. We exist according to His will. He is everywhere and in everything, and meanwhile, we also see Him as being "in heaven," in the world of the Spirit, the world of light and perfect completeness. This desirable and inexplicable world pours into us, into our lives. "Name"—His name is Love. The image of love is the Chalice, formed from light that rises above the horizon like the sun. "Thy Kingdom Come"—we wait and thirst for this Kingdom, but we are called to work for it. Continue in like manner to the end of the prayer, feeling each word and reflecting upon it.

Themes for meditating on God in times of inner silence can be varied, but here are a few examples:

1. *I am Your creation.* Sense that not one cell of your body belongs to you, but that everything you have was given to you—life itself and the Spirit. Realize that your existence is in God's hands and that you belong fully to Him.

2. *I thank the Lord.* Realize how the world was brought into existence from nothing and acknowledge how many gifts you have received. Thank God for

everything good in life, including trials. Thank Him for life, work, people, things, books, and the world. Thank Him for everything that surrounds you, feeds you, or gives you joy.

3. *The spirit rules over the flesh.* Realize that the highest gift in you is your spirit, which is by nature called to rule. God gave your spirit the same power over the flesh as He gave mankind over nature during creation (Gen. 1:26).

4. *He has given me* His *Spirit* (1 Jn. 4:13). Consider the intimate bond that exists between you and the I AM. Consider that you are made in His image and likeness. Consider that He wants to move in you.

5. *Thy will be done.* Fully submit "ourselves and each other" to His Providence.[68] Trust Him completely and hope for His help.

You can meditate upon words from Scripture, prayers, hymns, and the Liturgy.[69] In each case, you must be careful that your meditation does not get sidetracked. It must be closely connected to your concrete situation and personality. In this time of meditation, it should feel as if you are standing directly before God. It is very important to be aware of His presence. It is also critical in these minutes of meditation for no outside ideas to slip into your thoughts. Any beginner knows how difficult this is, but difficulties should not scare you or cause you to grow cold.

An examination of conscience is also part of spiritual meditation. This may be combined with your daily prayer rule, or it may be done at the end of the week. An examination of conscience must absolutely be done before confession (see Chapter Eleven and Appendix C).[70]

Topics for spiritual meditation may be taken not only from prayers and short sayings from Scripture, but also from certain moments in sacred history.[71] Saint John Chrysostom recommends that while meditating on themes from the Gospels, we specifically envision the situation and the details of events within the passage.[72] That being said, we must remember that people with well-developed imaginations could fall into "fantasizing"—the unhealthy excitement of the soul that an inexperienced person may confuse with authentic spiritual experience. Here, a danger lurks for the spiritual life—the potential dominance of emotional and even carnal elements that distort the internal order and lead to pathologies and false mysticism. In prayer and spiritual meditation, therefore, we must be extremely vigilant and must not abuse the resource of our imagination.[73]

CHAPTER EIGHT

PRAYER IN EVERYDAY LIFE

I F WE WANT AN ATMOSPHERE OF PRAYER TO FILL OUR LIVES MORE and more, we must not limit prayer to the time we spend standing in church or at home in front of icons, or sitting reading the Scriptures.[74] Prayer can make its way little by little into all corners of our everyday life. This is not easy to achieve, but the one who works toward frequent prayer receives tangible help from above. What different types and methods of frequent prayer are there?

The first way to practice frequent prayer is to *think about God*. When any person captures our heart and causes us to love him, our thoughts turn to him endlessly. The same thing happens to a person overtaken by the love of God. According to an expression of the psalms, such a person rejoices when he "remembers" God (see Ps. 42:4; 105:3–5). These thoughts about God have several aspects.

- We think about our relationship with Him. We are filled with trust, thankfulness, and feelings of repentance.
- We think of Him in light of His revelation. We meditate on His majesty, goodness, and love for mankind.
- We think about Him when we are faced with the question of how to fulfill His will. We say with Christ, "I do not seek My own will but the will of the Father who sent Me" (John 5:30).

Prayer before meals, either publicly or privately, also serves this goal of being reminded of God's presence. A well-known Russian priest of the nineteenth century, Father Rodion Putyatin, wrote,

> When we drink and eat with prayer and blessing, we
> drink and eat to the glory of God, and all that we do to
> His glory leads our soul to salvation. . . . With prayer
> and blessing, even wine can make our hearts glad with a
> spiritual joy, and physical bread can become salvific for
> our soul. . . . Even lowly animals know and remember
> the one who feeds them and gives them drink. . . . How
> then can we not know and remember Christ?[75]

We must learn to look at all things in light of their connection with God and to discover the spiritual significance of all creation. For example, when in a crowd of people, we should remember that we are surrounded by people for whom Christ shed His blood. Taking an infant into our arms, we need to remember that this child has been prepared to become the temple of the Holy Spirit. We should perceive a forest or river as God's message addressed to us. All of these are His creations, in which we can know *the presence* of the Creator, Who called them into being and sustains life in them to this day.

A thought in and of itself is always in danger of becoming impersonal and abstract. We know from experience, and psychologists remind us, that when our thoughts are expressed verbally, they become more clear and concrete. Words bring into action other internal mechanisms, allowing for a person's deeper participation in prayer. This is why it is so important for us to have *a conversation with God.*

We can talk with Him about everything that bothers us, including our attitude toward Him and toward others around us. We begin to thank Him, to make supplications, and to express our love to Him. The habit of turning to God as Father, Son, and Holy Spirit must be rooted within us. Then our prayer will not be abstract but will acquire the characteristic of a face-to-face conversation (see Exod. 33:11). In his diary, Father Alexander Elchaninov wrote, "If 'the Father knoweth' [see Matt. 6:8], why should we ask for anything, as we do in the Lord's Prayer and other prayers? What matters in such prayers is our act of turning consciously to God, our humility, the feeling of connection and dependence; and besides this, there is the importance of framing things explicitly in words, [the importance] of communion."[76]

Some people use different short prayers from the Bible each day; others repeat the same prayer for a whole week. You can write these short prayers out or take them from a prayer book. The Jesus Prayer is one such prayer (see Chapter Nine). To stay focused on one short prayer, it is very helpful to repeat it using a prayer rope.

Brother Lawrence, a seventeenth-century Carmelite lay monk, became a spiritual father to many of his contemporaries, instructing them in the practice of "entering oneself." In the course of the day, while performing his duties in the monastery's kitchen, he would from time to time enter into the depths of his own spirit for a few seconds. There, he would acquire peace and an awareness of God's presence.

Too often, we are so entangled in external activity that it paralyzes our spirits. Periodic detachment and the deep entrance into our spirits may become decisive factors in our spiritual life. The fifth-century saint John of Karpathos said, "So as not to be deceived and carried away by the vain and empty things that the senses bring before us, we should listen to the words of the prophet Isaiah: 'Come, my people, enter into your inner room'—the shrine of your heart, which is closed to every conception derived from the sensible world, that image-free dwelling-place illumined by dispassion and the overshadowing of God's grace."[77]

Constant reference to the Bible, especially to the Gospels, should become our vital necessity. When we open the Holy Scriptures, we stop the flow of chaotic thoughts and feelings, and it is as if we enter into the world of the Divine Word. This entrance is *already* prayer.

The practice of frequent prayer and of entering oneself does not require much time. Success depends on the frequency of such prayerful "minutes of peace." We need to get into the habit of using any free minute for this deep fellowship with God, whether it be just a moment as we transition from one task to another, as we walk or drive, or as we lie down or get up. We need to be able to interrupt our work in order to "catch sight of God."

An ancient wise man once said, "A day in which I have not helped anyone is a lost day." We should remind ourselves of these words often. Prayer, if not coupled with active love, risks degenerating into self-delusion. Serving others should be the same kind of daily activity as eating and drinking. Some of us have the opportunity to serve all the time; others must actively seek ways to serve. It is not necessary to list here all the ways to serve people. Enough lost, sad, needy, sick, and elderly people are surrounding us, and they are all waiting for help. The Lord says, "Inasmuch as you did it to one of the least of these My brethren, you did it to Me" (Matt. 25:40). That is why mutual service is essentially a form of worship and prayer. Let us remember once and for all that "faith by itself, if it does not have works, is dead" (Jas. 2:17).

CHAPTER NINE

THE HIGHEST STAGES OF PRAYER

A PERSON JUST BEGINNING A LIFE OF PRAYER MUST BE cautious about rushing into the highest forms of prayer. The harmonious and healthy unveiling of our inner spiritual strength should be completed one step at a time. One who ignores this due to impatience may fall victim to pride and a diseased condition. Therefore, these higher stages of prayer must stand before us as a desirable goal into which only the Lord Himself can lead us. In these stages, He reveals Himself in the depths of our spirit. We can only prepare the tilled soil for His sacred sowing. Yet, on the early paths, we can still see reflections of perfect prayer. Sometimes apart from our will, this prayer is sparked in our heart, bringing news from the promised land of the Spirit. In this chapter, I will touch very briefly on three of the highest forms of prayer: silent prayer, unceasing prayer, and the Jesus Prayer. Again and again, I will remind you that this is but a glimpse of the *future*, which depends upon God's gifts of grace and upon our readiness to receive them.

PRAYER IN SILENCE

Metropolitan Anthony says, "Inner silence is [the] absence of any sort of inward stirring of thought or emotion, but it is complete alertness, openness to God."[78] Minutes of inner peace, discussed earlier in Chapter Seven, can serve as thresholds to the preparation of the soul and spirit for this state. After a year of systematically completing the prayer rule and spiritual meditation, you may attempt to choose a time and place once a week in order to tune your spirit to be in full attentiveness to God's voice resounding in the silence. Here, all supplications and words are silenced and all that remains is reverent expectation. The smallest vibration of the body, soul, or spirit may become an obstacle to this silence. This is why it is necessary to constantly exercise control over your thoughts and emotions. If we achieve authentic silence from time to time, we must not count this toward our "successes." We must remember that the Spirit of God can visit a person who is not yet prepared, in order to encourage him to reach higher.

We should not despair if our efforts seem to be in vain, even if we lose the sense of God's presence. After all, we should not seek "excitement," but love for Christ. The desire to attain Him is to have already attained Him in some measure. But He Himself knows when it is necessary for us to sense His closeness. Therefore, we will wait patiently and humbly. If we stand fast through periods of dryness and spiritual barrenness, He will come to us and open the spring of silent prayer. This silent prayer will not depend upon us, but will flow like a quiet stream of grace.

PRAYER WITHOUT CEASING

Within us, a deep reality manifests itself in the form of unceasing prayer. Grace can turn this into a conscious "work." Any soul in a state of grace is immersed in a state of constant prayer. In the depths of his existence, a person feels a pull toward God. Yet, as a free being, he can resist this "spiritual gravity" and suppress the intimate prayer within him. If he does not block it, however, he is already on the right path.

Prayer without ceasing is compatible with human nature, for everything within us—everything that makes us human—comes from God and draws us to Him. The grace of the sacraments helps to awaken this innermost nature. In baptism, a Christian's spirit is sanctified and becomes a participant in the Divine nature (2 Pet. 1:4). A person's entire sanctified nature pursues the Creator. When this deep movement reaches his consciousness, he must submit to this innate pull toward God and joyfully respond to the One who is calling. The significance of unceasing prayer is to teach a person to follow his inborn desire for God.

The very same behaviors can have quite different motives and goals. The same work can be done simply for a wage or for the sake of one's family, or it can be animated by the desire to fulfill God's will. It is, therefore, not enough to just do good deeds. Let us remember the righteousness of the Pharisees mentioned in the Gospels. They were pious, yet their piety was filled not with sincere love toward God, but with vanity. There must also be an honorable direction in our prayers. God must stand in the forefront, not we ourselves. We need to constantly check the orientation of our will and purge it of such weeds as self-gratification, spiritual comfort, and vanity.

When the Lord sanctifies us with His gifts of grace, our secret prayer becomes conscious, and frequent prayer becomes unceasing prayer. This kind of gift can be given suddenly, when we least expect it, and it holds us in its wings over the course of several days or for a shorter or longer time. This is God's direct influence on our soul. After this, however, periods of dryness may come (see Chapter Six). These periods clearly show that the gift of grace originates from God.

THE JESUS PRAYER

The Jesus Prayer is a special type of deep prayer that has been known to Eastern ascetics since the fifth century. All who have introduced this prayer into their lives testify to its power. Metropolitan Anthony explains, "More than any other prayer, the Jesus Prayer aims at bringing us to stand in God's presence with no other thought but the miracle of our standing there and God with us, because in the Jesus Prayer there is nothing and no one except God and us."[79] This prayer requires great diligence and the ability to concentrate. Having such great power, this prayer can also become a danger to those who approach it without preparation. The holy fathers considered repentance and humility to be necessary conditions for this prayer. Archimandrite Paisius Velichkovsky writes, "According to Saint John Climacus and many other Holy Fathers, humility born from obedience allows the one praying to avoid all of the devil's deceptions and snares and to constantly exercise himself in this deed of the mind [the recitation of the Jesus Prayer] peacefully, silently, without any harm, and with great success for the soul."[80]

The prayer is expressed as follows: *Lord Jesus Christ, Son of God, have mercy on me, a sinner.* There is also a shortened version: *Lord Jesus, have mercy on me,* or *Jesus, Son of God, have mercy on me.* This invocation requires concentration, so that our mind "is not turned aside to any mental images," according to Blessed Diadochos of Photiki.[81]

Repetitions of the prayer must be limited to a specified number. A prayer rope is helpful in keeping track of this number. Saint Nicodemus of the Holy Mountain recommends beginning and ending one's regular prayer rule with several repetitions of the Jesus Prayer. He writes, "As to the number of times you should repeat this prayer and on what occasions, you should decide this yourself, or ask the advice of your spiritual Father. Only do not undertake too much at first, but increase the number of repetitions gradually, as your enjoyment of this prayer grows. If the desire comes to double the set number, do not deny it to yourself, but take it not as a set rule, but only for this occasion."[82]

The holy fathers warn against hurrying through this work of prayer, trying too hard, or impatiently looking for results.[83] Saint

Nicodemus continues: "You must know that true success comes within, unnoticeably, without ostentation, as is the case with the growth of the body. . . . Do not set a time for achievement in this prayer. Decide only one thing: to work, and to work. Months and years will go by before the first feeble indications of success begin to show."[84]

The body and the Jesus Prayer. Ascetics recommend a sitting position for exercises in the Jesus Prayer (see Chapter Five). This does not mean, however, that you cannot say the Jesus Prayer while working or walking, or in church.

The effects of the Jesus Prayer. According to Metropolitan Anthony, this prayer, concentrating on the name of Christ, "brings together all of a person's spiritual, psychological, and bodily powers in worship and love. In this way, it makes our existence steadfast."[85] In the fallen state, a person's nature is layered and divided. Anarchical thoughts and feelings make him unable to focus his mind on God. A person's *wholeness* is restored when "the mind descends into the heart," meaning that all spheres of this person are subject to his spirit. This "descent" facilitates the Jesus Prayer. A restoration of wholeness under the influence of this prayer appears on every level.

1. The Jesus Prayer helps to heal the body, trains us to control breathing, and strengthens psychological balance.
2. Through the Jesus Prayer, the life of the senses becomes more organized and increases control over thoughts and emotions.
3. The main result of the Jesus Prayer is seen in the area of the spirit. Concentration on the holy name of Christ permeates our entire spiritual life with light. The prayer takes over our entire existence.

The name *Jesus* (*Yeshua* in Aramaic) means "YHWH is salvation." To pronounce His name is to give yourself over to Christ, to open yourself up to Him, to participate in His life, and to put yourself under the influence of His saving and renewing love. His name has sanctifying power. If we sin, He forgives us. If we are tempted, He frees us. If we are thankful, He draws us to Himself. By repeating this name, we plug into the prayer of Christ Himself, enter into His relationship with the Father, and by the power of the Holy Spirit, Who is His Spirit, we find access to the Father's heart as his children.

To pronounce the name of Jesus is to confirm that Jesus is Lord; yet "no one can say that Jesus is Lord except by the Holy Spirit" (1 Cor. 12:3). Calling on the name of the Savior, we clothe ourselves in Jesus's submission to the Spirit. His name becomes the center from which the Spirit falls upon us, and, through us, upon our brothers and upon the whole world. As we see in Acts (2:21, 4:17, 8:12), in the power of this name, people come to faith and the Church is gathered.

The name of Jesus, by joining us to Him, not only allows us to enlarge His Mystical Body, the Church, but also leads us into its very core and binds us tightly with each of its members. As we honor the name of Jesus, we more fully live and feel as one with the Church and we contribute to its growth and unity. When co-laboring within the Church, we receive the opportunity to act within all of creation as well.

From the book of Acts, we know that the apostles healed people and performed many other miracles by the power of Jesus's name (Acts 3:16, 4:10). His name helps us to unleash the desire for God that is hiding, often imperceptibly, in people's hearts. It also gives us the power to awaken the Father's praises that sleep in the depths of the material world, which is in waiting (Rom. 8:19). When we proclaim the name of Jesus over the mountains and seas, over the plants and animals, over everything in the natural world, we give life to their mute and subconscious desire for God. Finally, the duty of the Christian is to call for Christ's coming on behalf of all creatures, people, and things—that by Him, all would be saved and brought to the Father in triumph (1 Cor. 15:24). The continual recitation of the Jesus Prayer is in accord with the final words and proclamation in the book of Revelation: "Come, Lord Jesus" (Rev. 22:20).

Finally, it is necessary once again to emphasize that these highest stages and forms of prayer are, for the majority of us, tasks for the future. We should not skip the beginning stages to pursue the very highest. This would lead to nothing but sad consequences. Let us rely on humility, which is a guarantee of health for the soul and spirit. Let us pray in anticipation of the coming of the Lord into our souls, at which time grace, and not we ourselves, will create within us a life of prayer.

PART THREE
PRAYER AND GREAT LENT

CHAPTER TEN

THE PRAYER OF SAINT EPHREM
OF SYRIA

໐໐

This chapter is an excerpt from Father Alexander's lecture "Great Lent,"
delivered on April 1, 1989, at the Krasnaya Presnya Club in Moscow.

PRAYER OF SAINT EPHREM OF SYRIA

O Lord and Master of my life,
Take from me the spirit of sloth, despair, lust of power, and idle talk.*

But give rather the spirit of chastity, humility, patience, and love to Thy servant.*

Yea, O Lord and King,
Grant me to see my own transgressions, and not to judge my brother,
For blessed art Thou, unto ages of ages. Amen.*

* prostration

ON EVERY DAY OF GREAT LENT, EXCEPT FOR SATURDAYS and Sundays, we read the prayer "O Lord and Master of my life."[86] According to tradition, this prayer was written in the fourth century in Syria by the ascetic Mar-Ephrem, or as we are accustomed to calling him, Ephrem of Syria. A Syriac monk, poet, and theologian, Ephrem entered the realm of world literature as a famous author and one of the glorious sons of the Syriac Church.

"O Lord and Master of my life." He is the King of my life. The One who gave me life. The One who is the center and focus of my life.

"Take from me the spirit of sloth." Sloth is laziness. According to an ancient saying, this is the mother of all vices. Laziness seems like such a harmless thing, but it gives birth to much darkness and evil.[87]

"Take from me the spirit of . . . despair." Christianity is a joyous teaching, joyous! So the one who despairs has walked away from it. Seraphim of Sarov, a great Russian saint from the beginning of the nineteenth century, said, "We must not despair, for Christ saved all."[88]

"Take from me the spirit of . . . lust of power." This means the love of power. Everyone has this. Do not think that this is the kind of thing that, like the cult of personality, is only in politics. This can happen in families or in any small community. Every person carries within himself the seed of ambition to suppress another's will, to choke it, and to bring it into submission.

"Take from me the spirit of . . . idle talk." Let's be honest with ourselves. How long do we all have left to live? Not long at all. Therefore, I stress that we must appreciate life, love this gift that God has given us, and remember that we take into eternity only that which is in our hearts. Idle talk and chatter are terrible, signifying the killing of time. I make an exception for children. Children have the right to chatter up to the age of 15 or 16. When children talk, they are learning how to socialize and are developing their language. But when these "children" are twenty or even over forty, they are only being merciless to themselves.

The prayer continues: "But give rather the spirit of chastity, humility, patience, and love to Thy servant. . . ." "Chastity" is purity in relationship to the world and people. It is a wholeness of the soul. It means you are undivided, so that the passions have no control over you.

"Humility" is the wisdom of a healthy person.[89] Humility in this case is to know that you take a back seat to eternity. Do not puff yourself up like the frog in Krylov's fable—it popped![90] Do not get puffed up, but know your worth. The wisdom of modesty is rare and wonderful. The wisdom of modesty is not an exaggerated humility that is worse than pride, but it is rather a healthy soul. When a person begins to imagine that he is something he is not, he is just a few steps away from delusions of grandeur and a pathological state of pride. As soon as one person announces that he is a member of the Council of Ministers or that he is Napoleon, he is put in the psych ward. Another might not say such a thing, so he's not in the hospital, but in his soul, he thinks he is above everyone else.

"Patience." What is patience, or long-suffering? It is not the state of cattle that simply endure everything. It is absolutely not the humiliation of a person. It is certainly not a compromise with evil. Patience is the ability to keep an undisturbed spirit in those situations that otherwise do not allow for such tranquility. Long-suffering is the ability to go for the goal even when you encounter various obstacles along the way. Long-suffering is the ability to maintain a joyful spirit in the midst of great amounts of sadness. Long-suffering is to have victory and to overcome. Real long-suffering is a form of bravery.

And finally, "love." Love is the highest happiness of mankind. It is the ability of our souls to be open (philosophers use the term *immanent*) and thus to be internally available for another person. When riding the escalator on your way to take the subway, check to see if you are able to love or not. When you look at those people going in the opposite direction, and they disgust you, it means that every corner of your soul is plugged up and any feeling of love that you have is still in its embryonic state. The power of Christ's grace, however, is able to rebuild a person in such a way that he would see people completely differently. This reconfiguration would make it possible for his first reaction to be one of good will. Such a change would allow him to immediately see beauty—spiritual beauty in an attractive woman or man—even where others do not notice it. Christ's grace makes it possible for a changed person, when he sees a suffering face, to feel compassion. And it allows him to be open. Such a person is always happy, because he is in unity with people. He lives by love.

The end of the prayer says, "Yea, O Lord and my King, grant me to see my own transgressions, and not to judge my brother." This is likely understandable to you all. The best remedy for being judgmental is to be able to criticize oneself. We are often exceptionally attentive, observant, and even psychologically attuned to the sins of our neighbor. In this, we demonstrate our maximum knowledge of all moral commandments in great detail. But we behave as a strict judge, not having the right to do so, for we are guilty of the very things for which we judge others. You may ask me, "Well, isn't that just dangerous peacemaking[91] and a compromise with evil?" In no way is this so. We should always call evil by its name. But toward the person who has fallen into this sin, we must have compassion.

This, then, is the essence of the Prayer of Saint Ephrem, which is read every day during Great Lent with prostrations.

CHAPTER ELEVEN

THE OBSERVANCE OF GREAT LENT

ᚼᚹᚷᚹᚷᚼ

The editors of the second Russian edition wrote, "We considered it appropriate to supplement the first edition by adding the handbook, 'On the Observance of Great Lent,' which is useful for those who are newly baptized or new to the [Russian Orthodox] Church. This handbook was circulated in several typewritten copies during Father Alexander's lifetime. It offers an extremely abbreviated form of the foundational Christian teachings on this important season, providing a knowledge without which one's prayer life cannot achieve fullness." Father Alexander thus wrote this chapter with an intended audience of newly baptized Russian Orthodox believers. We hope that it will still prove instructive for Western Christians, and even for the seasoned Orthodox Christian.

THE CHURCH HAS SPECIALLY PROVIDED THE TIME OF GREAT Lent so we can gather our thoughts, so we can focus, and so we can prepare ourselves to greet the day of *Pascha* (Easter).[92] By way of Great Lent, we must try to grow in what is lacking and to fill in the blanks within our spiritual lives, which have suffered so much due to life's messes, distractions, and laziness.

GENERAL RULES

1. Abstaining from meat is a must. Any other rules can be discussed with a spiritual leader. In addition, it is good to choose a particular, everyday thing from which to abstain during these days, continuing until *Pascha*.

2. During the fast, you should read all four Gospels.

3. Refrain from all superfluous meetings and activities—from all that distracts. You do not need to abandon relaxation, of course, but you should choose such forms of relaxation that do not disturb the peace in your soul. Good examples would be walks and trips to the countryside, etc.

4. Read the Prayer of Saint Ephrem of Syria every day, preferably in a meditative fashion by which you concentrate on the meaning of the words. You should meditate mainly on one part of the prayer. For example, you could focus on the phrase "Lord and Master of my life" or on Christ as the Alpha and Omega of your life—its purpose, love, and goal. Feel this section of the prayer for at least a short moment.

5. In addition to the Prayer of Saint Ephrem, dedicate at least ten minutes every day to prayerful meditation—five minutes in the morning and five minutes in the evening. This is a minimum; thirty minutes total (fifteen in the morning, fifteen in the evening) would be better. It is important not to miss even one day throughout Great Lent.

   Select a comfortable place and a comfortable position for prayer. If this is not possible, do not simply skip this time. You can meditate while walking, while at work, in the evening when all others have fallen asleep, or in the morning. In short, adapt to the situation. It is extremely important that nothing "presses in on you," that the necessity to do something urgently does not cause worry, and that fatigue does not overcome you.

Before starting your prayerful meditation, cross yourself or mentally call on God's name. Force yourself to set aside all cares (this is the most difficult aspect) and, exerting your will, put yourself in God's presence. Realize that wherever you may be, you are always with Him, in His presence. After this, turn your gaze to an icon or the cross. If you are not at home, close your eyes partially and envision the image of the cross. It is necessary that your whole body acquire a state of peace, that your breathing not be rushed, and that you remain still (aside from the sign of the cross). After this, mentally say a phrase from a prayer or from the Gospel (or you could choose a phrase from a litany, an *akathist* [hymn], or the Liturgy) and try to hold it in your mind for as long as possible—contemplating it, diving into its depths, and feeling its multifaceted connection to your life. In the beginning, this will be difficult. Perhaps only by the third week will things improve.

Most importantly, never give up. Continue this every day of the fast for five minutes in the morning and five minutes in the evening. If you must, you can vary the time, but it is better to choose a specific time and stick to it. You need not be surprised or discouraged if you find that you are distracted and are unable to concentrate. It is helpful to consider yourself a beginning student who is coming to prayerful meditation for the first time. It is good to make a list of prayerful sayings a week in advance. Throughout the day, you should try to return your thoughts to the topic of meditation in any spare moments from work, as if you were preparing for a meeting. The key to success is to achieve inner silence, which is the most difficult thing to do in our noisy age.

6. After a five-minute meditation, sit or stand silently and attentively, as if you were listening to the silence. Then, with this silence in your heart, return to work, trying to preserve this "sound" as long as possible.

7. Every Sunday during Great Lent, attend the Liturgy and be on time for the service. Before the service while the Hours are being read, it is good to say this prayer:

I believe, Lord;
Establish my faith.
I hope in you, Lord;
Strengthen my hope.
I have loved you, Lord;
Purify my love and kindle it.
I am broken, Lord;
But increase my repentance.
I honor You, Lord, my Creator;
I groan for You and call on You.
　　　Direct me by Your wisdom;
　　　　　Protect me and strengthen me.
I surrender my intentions to You, my God;
May they come from You.
May my deeds be done in Your name
And my desires in Your will.
Enlighten my mind, strengthen my will;
Purify my body, sanctify my soul.
May I see my transgressions,
That I may not stumble in pride;
Help me to overcome temptation.
May I glorify You
All the days of this life You have given to me.
Amen.[93]

Establish with a spiritual leader the frequency with which you partake of Communion, but you must prepare yourself ahead of time for Communion on Great Thursday (Maundy Thursday), the day of the Last Supper.

1. During the fast, it is especially important to increase your prayers for others. You should not miss any chance to pray for someone who is sick, in despair, or going through difficult trials. You need to pray for him without delay, as time and strength allows.

2. Make a list of particularly venerable saints and, over the course of the fast, turn to them more frequently, as to the living, as to helpers and friends (see Chapter Twelve). Light candles for them, and pray before their icons.

3. Beware of inconsistency: highs and lows. A calm and systematic rhythm of prayerful meditation will protect you from inconsistency. In the case of excessive spiritual excitement, you should bridle yourself. Remember that it is often the passions that are participating in this spiritual excitement, and not the spirit. Keeping this in mind will help you to be on guard for pitfalls.

THE WEEKS OF THE FAST DURING GREAT LENT

THE FIRST WEEK

Perform the following cycle of prayerful meditation:

Day 1: *The Day of Ecclesiastes*

Meditate on the vanity of everything earthly. A person at the height of glory, having achieved much, will die like the rest, and occasionally with more difficulty. What was it all for? Some walked among corpses, others killed their own souls; in the end, it all came to nothing. Read the prayer "What Sweetness of Life" (see Appendix D). Meditate on how honor, love, glory, and health are all insignificant and empty if one is without a spiritual life! All of it tumbles down like a waterfall into the pool of death. Everything bears the seal of imperfection. All that we run after and all that we cling to is but smoke and dust. Everything is meaningless—terrifyingly meaningless and sinister.[94]

Day 2: "Out of the depths I have cried" (Psalm 130)

I have so often served various idols. I have so many illusions and so much futility in my life. I so passionately set my heart on things I cannot keep. In my ambitions, my love of praise, and my futility, I had not realized what lowly motives fueled me or what a deep hole I had dug, but now I see it. I am helpless to do anything to fix myself. I am already doomed in this life to be in a hell of unmet desires and in slavery to the elements of the flesh and to the sin of pride. I am a complete nothing.

This is not a form of false pride but an honest view of ourselves. Let us remember our dreams that often speak of our wild, hidden desires, to which we close our eyes. Let us acknowledge that we cannot control our own nature.

Day 3: The Good News

Yet there is a way out. Salvation is open to me if I will again return to Christ. Christ is my Good News. He was born for me, so that I might come alive and be healed. He taught me. He revealed Himself to me as God—God the Savior. Only with His help can I stand up on my feet.

Day 4: Healing

Christ heals me through His death. His cross and blood were for me, for all of us who do not have the strength to enter onto the right path, even though we see it. He showed us the Way (the Sermon on the Mount), the Truth (God meets us where we are), and the Life (life with Him).

Day 5: Thanksgiving

I gradually come to life. I am infinitely thankful to Him for stretching out His hand to me. And now there is no end to my gratitude for

everything: for life, for salvation, for joy, for trials, for people, for the
world, for every little thing. It all comes from God. I open the doors
of my house, expecting that He will come under the roof of my soul.

Day 6: *Examination of Conscience*

I must prepare my house and check it in anticipation of my Guest's
arrival. I take the lamp of His commandments into my hands to
illuminate the dark corners. Dust, dirt, and clutter are everywhere.
The more I illuminate things, the gloomier the picture becomes. But
I will not despair. I will patiently begin to clean. I will check my
conscience slowly and step-by-step against the Ten Commandments
and against the Sermon on the Mount. This is my preparation for
confession. On Sunday, there will be many people at church, so
there will be a general confession. Hence, I must carefully consider
everything beforehand, so I can at least bring a general confession to
the Lord (see Appendix C).

Day 7: *Communion*

This is a day of intense gratitude. Let us make a vow to God to do
something in His name as a sign of our thankfulness.

THE SECOND WEEK
THE WEEK OF THE TRIUMPH OF ORTHODOXY

This week, along with general spiritual exercises, I require myself
to do something special for the church (cleaning, singing, helping
with the candles, teaching, or something else).

THE THIRD WEEK
THE WEEK OF SAINT GREGORY PALAMAS

Since this week is dedicated to the holy *hesychast* (silent monk)
Gregory Palamas, make a promise not to speak even one unnecessary
word this week. Christian families must make an agreement to be
silent. One who is the only believer in his or her family should try to

do this as best as possible. No conversations, not even good ones, are allowed, not to mention unnecessary ones. Only those conversations that are necessary in order to function are allowed. They say "an angel flies by" whenever there is a moment of silence, so our task this week is not to allow him to leave. For some, silence will be difficult, but this is mainly due to the fact that we all talk too much. Those who find it very difficult should accept it as a cross and penance.

THE FOURTH WEEK
THE WEEK OF THE VENERATION OF THE CROSS

This week is dedicated to meditations on the cross and the significance of our cross-bearing. Any difficulty, if met with desperate protest on our part, is not a cross. It becomes a cross when we try to bear it "with agreement," if not voluntarily.

THE FIFTH WEEK
THE WEEK OF SAINT JOHN CLIMACUS

The most dangerous thing to do on the spiritual ladder is to look back to see how far you have come. There is no room for "tracking your progress" here, for if you were to experience success, you would soon also experience self-satisfaction, which would completely negate all previous efforts. You must consider yourself always to be on the first step. God can raise you up to the tenth step at any time. Symptoms of complete failure include a constantly depressed mood or abrupt swings from ecstasy to despair.

THE SIXTH WEEK
THE WEEK OF SAINT MARY OF EGYPT

Saint Mary of Egypt is for us an example of repentance. This week, we try to gather our thoughts and write down a confession for our whole lives. We must be strict with ourselves, not missing anything and looking into all aspects of our lives. It is good to dedicate Lazarus

Saturday to meditation on death and to making preparations for death, according to the writings of Saint Francis de Sales.[95]

HOLY WEEK[96]

Read the prescribed passage from the Gospels for each day. If you have access to a book about Christ's life, read from it.[97] On Great Thursday, attend general confession and take Communion. Remember that this is a special participation in the Last Supper. Mentally follow Christ into Great Friday. During this week, the Roman Catholic Church reads fourteen prayers before images of Christ's Passion, called the Stations of the Cross. These images are specially hung around the walls of the sanctuary. In lieu of this, we can use icons or simply follow Christ's journey in our mind. Texts for meditation are usually provided in Western prayer books.

Go with God! May you spend the Great Fast with great diligence. May you greet Christ's resurrection with joy!

PART FOUR

PRAYER AND THE COMMUNION OF SAINTS

Since we are surrounded by so great a cloud of witnesses,
Let us lay aside every weight, and the sin which so easily ensnares us,
And let us run with endurance the race that is set before us.

—Hebrews 12:1

CHAPTER TWELVE

THE SAINTS AND PRAYER
SELECTED SERMONS

ΩΩ

Unless otherwise noted, the sermons in this chapter come from Father Alexander's sermon series "Feast Days Dedicated to Saints and Commemorative Days." Most of these sermons were delivered between the late 1970s and the late 1980s.[98]

❀ FULFILLING YOUR OBLIGATIONS ❀

Excerpt from a sermon on the commemoration of Saint Philip, Metropolitan of Moscow. The editors of the second Russian edition wrote, "Father Alexander especially loved and venerated this saint, and not only because St. Philip is commemorated on his birthday (January 22). In St. Philip, Father Alexander saw an example of a great feat done by a clergyman who resolved to fight alone against a [tyrannical] regime."

. . . In the history of Russia, there were two points when tyranny—the rule of an insane and cruel person over masses of people—reached its limit. These were during the time of Tsar Ivan (whom the people called "the Terrible") and during the rule of Stalin, who loved and was fascinated by Ivan the Terrible. Stalin felt a kindred spirit across the centuries with this executioner of the people. . . .

When Philip came to Moscow, Tsar Ivan greeted him kindly and warmly, but Philip first said, "If you want me to work here in Moscow for the Church, then give me the right to mourn." At that time, *to mourn* meant to intercede before the tsar on behalf of those who are repressed. The tsar was shaken, but he agreed. Thus, only on this condition did Philip accept the white *kukol* [cowl] of the Metropolitan of Moscow. And his ministry began. . . .

When Philip became the head of the Russian Orthodox Church, he thereby took upon himself the obligation of being a witness. The metropolitan gathered the high-ranking clergy to a council and began to consult with them about how to bridle the tsar's lawlessness. No one supported Philip, however, because they were all intimidated. They were silent and scared. . . .

In Zagorsk[99] at the Moscow Theological Academy, a nineteenth-century painting depicts the holy metropolitan standing on his knees before an icon.[100] Graying, thin, and troubled, he turns to the icon with only one hope in God's justice. Right then, the door opens, and Maliuta Skuratov barges into the metropolitan's cell in his black headdress. He demands, "Bless me in my unrighteous deed!" But no! It was impossible to intimidate Philip, so Maliuta threw himself at him, and suffocated him with a pillow. . . . That is how Metropolitan Philip's life ended.

Soon after that, Ivan the Terrible died at a relatively young age; he wasn't even 60. By the time he died, he had unintentionally killed one of his own sons in a fit of rage, had lost many of those close to him, had lost a war, and was in deep loneliness and bitter misery. His memory remains blackened, the way it has always been with those who torture people.

Yet the Church glorified Philip as a saint. After many centuries, he is still a great example and a model for us of the steadfast fulfillment of one's obligations in any circumstances, for life is short. If you do not fulfill your obligations in this life, is it really worth living?

We all know very well that man is weak, that he does not always feel he has enough strength to completely fulfill his obligation. But we remember the saints and ask them to pray for us. We ask them to pray that our only Intercessor, our only Lord and Savior would lift us up from the dust. We ask them to pray that by the power of His love and grace—and not by our power—He would make us servants of His righteousness and His truth.

Amen.

☧ IMITATING CHRIST ☧

Excerpt from a sermon to commemorate the transfer of the relics of the hieromartyr Ignatius the God-Bearer [Ignatius of Antioch].

. . . When the first persecutions against faith in Christ began, a battalion of Roman soldiers brought into the capital [Rome] a person doomed to be put to death. His name was Ignatius, and he was one of the first bishops of Antioch, a city in Syria. He was a disciple of the apostles. He personally knew John the Theologian [the Apostle John], the Apostle Peter, and others among the earliest disciples of Christ. . . .

We are not really surprised at this person's fortitude and exceptional bravery. He was, after all, a saint! Yet, let us keep in mind that he was not only a saint, but he was also a man with infirmities and human weaknesses. And what awaited him? A disgraceful death in the Roman circus arena! . . .

Of course, things were not easy for him in those exhausting days and weeks. Where did he find strength? His strength is explained by one word alone, the nickname given to him, The God-Bearer. He carried Christ in his heart. And today, on the day of his commemoration, he calls each one of us to stand in imitation of him, the Bearer of God. Having been baptized into Christ, we have put on Christ.[101] We can take on His image, and, imitating the Lord, we can walk in His steps. We can walk in the steps of bravery and patience, in the steps of good works and self-control, in the steps of love for God and love for people. Only then, when we have fully acquired Christ in our hearts, can we say that we are His disciples.

Behold! Bishop Ignatius, when he was already doomed to become a martyr, says, "I am only now becoming a disciple. I am not yet a real Christian. I am just now learning this. I pray that I will be worthy of this calling."[102] All the more do we need to ask the Lord to help us to become His true disciples—not just people who come to church once a week and go home, remaining the same old pagans, but true bearers of Christ, God-bearers in our life, thoughts, feelings, deeds, and faith. And we will pray to the hieromartyr Ignatius, that by his example he would strengthen us, and that by his prayers he would encourage us on the path of following after Christ.

☙ LIVING FOR OTHERS ❧

Excerpt from a sermon on the day of commemoration for
Saint Nicholas the Wonderworker, Archbishop of Myra

. . . Certain saints did not bring glory to themselves during their lives, but they continue to pray for their brothers and to perform acts of charity in this world. Why is this so? It is because of the way this person lived—the works he did, the aspects on which he exerted his effort, and the priorities to which he committed his entire being throughout the course of his life.

We each live for ourselves, with our own worries. . . . Our very short life passes by, and then we are taken to the graveyard. In one or two generations, we will be forgotten. The epitaph on a tombstone does not always remain legible; everything becomes overgrown. . . . So let us keep in mind that after one hundred or two hundred years, the cemetery may still be there, but who will remember our grave after such a long period of time? We leave this life without a trace, and we only ask the Lord to give rest to our unfortunate and weak souls in the place He has prepared for us [John 14:2–3]. We wait for the future work of His Holy Spirit—that He would raise us who are sleeping in the grave and revive us.

So it is with us, but not with the great saints. We live for ourselves, but they so completely lived for others that when their earthly life had ended, the Lord gave them the power to continue to stay in this world, as if He raised them even before the general resurrection [Acts 24:15]. This is why remembering the saints is for us more than just remembering their deeds, their feats, and their holiness, but also their living influence on us. When we ask Nicholas the Wonderworker for help or healing, we talk to him as if he were alive and in our midst. Such is the grace of the saints who have given themselves to people.

A choice remains for us in this life. If we want to take the human path, the path of self-love and sin, then our reward will be sleep, nothingness, and absentminded prayer. Only later will the Lord revive us. Yet if, from the very first moments after our death, we want the Lord to give us the power to continue doing something in this life, we must try to live differently now—to live a Christian life.

Everyone knows who Saint Nicholas is! We also know a great many people from our own times who have died, but their lives were such that the Lord gave them this miraculous power to be seemingly immortal even before the general resurrection—just as He gave this power to Saint Nicholas. And such people pray for us and show us a multitude of signs and wonders, no less than those in ancient times.

Again, if we ask Nicholas the Wonderworker now for prayers and for help, we should consider not only asking for something, but also giving something, by doing something human, divine, and Christian in our life. Then, though only in the smallest, one-thousandths, most miniscule way, we will become like our great brothers—the saints, who shine both in their lives and after their bodily deaths.

Amen.

⊚ SPIRITUAL ENLIGHTENMENT ⊚

*Excerpt from a sermon on the day of commemoration for
Saint Tikhon of Zadonsk, Bishop of Voronezh and the
Wonderworker of Zadonsk.*

In the name of the Father, and of the Son, and of the Holy Spirit!

Today, the Holy Church celebrates the memory of the great Russian saint Tikhon of Zadonsk. In Russia, all people who love and value spiritual books on the Christian life know the name of Saint Tikhon of Zadonsk, who left for us the great treasure of his writings.

On the day of his commemoration, it is tradition to read the Gospel passage where the Lord calls us all to be the light of the world. Not only does He say, "I am the light of the world" (John 8:12),[103] but He also says to us—people following His path, taking up His cross, and believing in His gospel—"You are the light of the world" (Matt. 5:14)!

What a great responsibility and what a great calling for each of us! As it turns out, the Lord wants us to shine for this world—to shine with goodness and truth, with courage and service. In life's gloom and in the darkness of human grief, sin, and delusion, we believers must shine like a candle on a candlestick.

Tikhon of Zadonsk was that kind of light. . . . His older brother did everything possible so that the young Timothy (Tikhon's worldly name) could have a start in life, receive an education, and enter seminary. At seminary, he unexpectedly exhibited such amazing abilities that he astounded those who had been educated from a young age. It was not only his wisdom, his education, and his knowledge of many languages that astounded them, but also the light that shone from this young man, who became a teacher of Latin and philosophy.

At the age of thirty-four, he was tonsured into monasticism. Soon after, he became a monk-priest (hieromonk) and later a bishop. He was a man of such terrible health and was often so weak that he could not even walk without assistance from others. He served as a bishop for only four years. The rest of the time, he had to stay at home and rest, almost like a hermit. So as not to forsake his ministry, he wrote books. . . .

All four years of his episcopal service, Saint Tikhon of Zadonsk tried to root out paganism. He set this as his first priority. This may seem strange, since he lived just over 200 years ago, in the eighteenth century. One would think that paganism would have already been gone in Zadonsk, where he was bishop. Everyone was baptized and, of course, they all went to church on Sundays and other Feast days. Yet, the piercing eyes of Saint Tikhon saw that this was all just external packaging. He quickly figured out that his priests did not know God's Word and often served the Liturgy without understanding what they were doing. Laypeople were in an even more dreadful and dark ignorance.

So Tikhon of Zadonsk made it his job to re-teach the gospel to these people as long as he had enough strength. After entering the hermitage, he continued to do this with a quill in his hand. One of his main books is called *On True Christianity*.[104] Look at these telling and suggestive words: "On true Christianity!" So many other kinds of Christianity exist—fake Christianity, shallow Christianity, outward Christianity, and outward piety. The Lord compared such outward piety with a beautiful whitewashed tomb, within which lay decaying bones (see Matt. 23:27). Tikhon of Zadonsk also condemned it. Following in the footsteps of the prophets in the Holy Scriptures and of the Lord Himself, Tikhon called his fellow citizens and contemporaries (and us as well) to make their faith and Christianity internal and heartfelt. . . .

The saints continue to pray for those they have left behind in this life. On this day of Tikhon's commemoration, therefore, let us ask him who stands like a candle and a light in this world to edify us, to strengthen us, and to teach each of us to fulfill the will of Christ the Savior, who said, "Let your light so shine before men, that they may see your good works and glorify your Father in heaven!" (Matt. 5:16).

Amen.

❧ PRAYER TO THE THEOTOKOS ❧

Excerpt from a sermon during the Feast of the Meeting of Our Lord,
from the sermon cycle for the Twelve Great Feasts.

In the name of the Father, and of the Son, and of the Holy Spirit!

The Feast of the Meeting is considered a feast of both Christ and the Virgin Mary, the most pure Mother of God. On this day, the infant Jesus met the Old Testament face-to-face, so to speak. He met Simeon, an old man who, on the verge of leaving this life, said good-bye to it and thanked God, saying, "Lord, now You are letting Your servant depart in peace" (see Lk. 2:29). The ancient ways were passing, and a new work was just beginning.

Yet at the same time the Mother of the Lord heard strange words that neither she nor Joseph initially understood. The two even seemed confused. The elder Simeon took the Infant into his arms and said, "Behold, this Child is destined for the fall and rising of many in Israel, and for a sign which will be spoken against (yes, a sword will pierce through your own soul also), that the thoughts of many hearts may be revealed" (Lk. 2:34–35). In other words, the Mother of God would be tested in her heart through her Son. With this, Simeon foretold her suffering from the very beginning. . . .

Thus, many say that it was as if the Lord's Mother were crucified in her heart with Him. Her entire life, from the time she was called to become His Mother, was a Way of the Cross. This is why, when we remember the prophecy of the elder Simeon today, we bow to the wounds of her heart and her soul and to her Way of the Cross, and we cry,

Mother of God!
Pray for us suffering, burdened sinners,
Who also have a choice
Whether the Lord will be destined
For our falling or for our rising.

Let it be so! May her prayer uplift us. May we keep our faith through
all temptations and cruel trials, as she kept her faith on Golgotha and
at her Son's tomb.

We often stand at the graves of our friends and family, but also at
the graves of our hopes, our pillars of support, and our earthly human
designs. There is much we must bury, and then comes the hour of
despair, weak faith, and dismay. But if we remember the Cross of the
Mother of God, we will again hear God's voice and will get back up,
stand tall, and say,

Lord!
Just as Your Mother,
While walking after You, steadfast and hopeful,
Hid holy words in Her heart,
So we too will hide these words,
That in the dark hours of life,
They would strengthen us and give us power.
Amen.

CHAPTER THIRTEEN

FATHER ALEXANDER'S PUBLIC PRAYERS

✿

This chapter is a collection of various prayers spoken publicly by Father Alexander, whether in informal gatherings of parishioners or at the end of his sermons. Parishioners transcribed these from recorded talks and sermons, and they were eventually gathered together as a source of encouragement for other believers.[105]

A PRAYER FOR UNITY

✦ Lord Jesus Christ! You told us,
"Wherever two or three are gathered in My name,
There I am in their midst."

You did not desire for people to walk through this life alone.
You gathered us, so that we would be one family.

May we fulfill Your new commandment,
That we may love one another as You have loved us.
Give us patience, tolerance, and self control.

May we, through Your prayer and commandment, be one,
As You are one with the Father and the Spirit;
So that our light, which comes from You, would shine in this
    dark world,
And so that people would come to know Your love
In the love of the Father,

In the salvation of the Son,
And in the communion of the Holy Spirit.
Amen.

A PRAYER OF CHRIST'S DISCIPLES[106]

Jesus Christ, Son of God,
Who has shown us the Heavenly Father,
May we be Your disciples.

You promised to give peace to our souls,
But You do not desire negligent servants.
Give us the strength to stand watch and to stay awake.

May we be faithful to You, and to You alone.
Teach us to do everything in Your presence.
Make us Your children.

Give us the strength to fulfill Your will and Your covenant.
Teach us to do good.
Protect us from the yeast of the Pharisees.

Teach us to see what is important in life, to see only what is
    necessary.
Help us to be free from sin, idleness, and laxity of spirit.

Let everything that is good and wonderful in this world remind
    us of You.
Let the evil of this world be a warning to us.

May we see in sinners a mirror of our own iniquities.
Teach us to see brothers in those who think differently than we do,
In those of other confessions, and in unbelievers.

Let us remember how short life is,
So that the memory of our mortality
Would be the force behind our work and ministry.
Instill within us the ability to forgive, to love, and to give.
Teach us to live in prayer.
Let us now be participants in Your Kingdom.

Teach us to hate sin, but not the sinner.
Give us the power to testify about You.
Let us not be vain, petty, or shallow.

May You be our Alpha and Omega in this life and in eternity.
May we be Your disciples.
Amen.

A PRAYER FOR HUMILITY

Lord, have mercy! Christ, have mercy!
Jesus, gentle and humble in heart, hear me and have mercy on
  me.
Heavenly Father, God, have mercy on us!
Son, Redeemer of the world, have mercy on us!
Holy Spirit of God, have mercy on us!

Jesus, deliver me from the desire to avoid offenses against me!
Jesus, deliver me from the desire to force my own opinion!
Jesus, deliver me from the desire for people to take my advice!
Jesus, deliver me from the desire to be praised!
Jesus, deliver me from the desire to be respected!
Jesus, deliver me from the desire to be first!
Jesus, deliver me from the desire to be loved!

From the fear of being forgotten, deliver me, Jesus!

From the fear of being under suspicion, deliver me, Jesus!

From the fear of being unknown, deliver me, Jesus!

From the fear of being misunderstood, deliver me, Jesus!

From the fear of being rejected, deliver me, Jesus!

From the fear of being slandered, deliver me, Jesus!

From the fear of being humiliated, deliver me, Jesus!

From the fear of being mocked, deliver me, Jesus!

When others are appreciated more than I,

Help me, Jesus, to bear it in love!

When others are accepted, but I am forgotten,

Help me, Jesus, to bear it in love!

When my birthright is given to another,

Help me, Jesus, to bear it in love!

When others are considered more upright than I,

Help me, Jesus, to bear it in love!

When others are loved more than I,

Help me, Jesus, to bear it in love!

That I would not seek a high position,

Jesus, give me grace, humility, and love!

That I may readily do unpleasant duties unto Your glory,

Jesus, give me grace, humility, and love!

That I may see God's will in the orders of my superiors,

Jesus, give me grace, humility, and love!

That I may forgive in deed and not only in word,

Jesus, give me grace, humility, and love!

That I may treat everyone with love, especially those who
condemn me,

Jesus, give me grace, humility, and love!

That I may be quick to show contrition,

Jesus, give me grace, humility, and love!
That I would love poverty and indignity,
Jesus, give me grace, humility, and love!

Lamb of God, who took upon Yourself the sins of the world,
Forgive us, Lord!
Lamb of God, who took upon Yourself the sins of the world,
Hear us, Lord!
Lamb of God, who took upon Yourself the sins of the world,
Have mercy on us, Lord!

Jesus, gentle and humble in heart,
Hear my supplications and grant them according to Your mercy,
That I would joyfully agree to live unnoticed in this world
And that in my joy would be Your Glory and Love!
Amen.

MORNING PRAYER

Lord, may all that I do today be to your glory!
May all of my thoughts and desires be according to your will!

MORNING PRAYER

Lord, bless my prayer,
Help me to stand undistracted before You with all my soul and
body.
Teach me to pray to You.
Strengthen me in faith.
Give me a fervent love for You.

Lord, sanctify all of my thoughts, feelings, and deeds.
Teach me to discern Your will in every situation
And give me the strength to fulfill it.
Shut my mouth to evil and idle talk
And keep my hands from foolish deeds.
If adversity comes,
give me the strength to accept it unshakably
And to turn it into a sacrifice to You.

Lord, make me a wellspring of goodness for everyone I encounter
    today.
Accept my prayer for those who do not know You
And deliver them from unbelief.

I thank You, Lord, for my soul,
For everything that surrounds me:
For those near and far,
For heaven and earth,
And, above all, for Your life-giving love.

Help me, Lord, to remember You and thank You all day long.
Amen.

A PRAYER FOR WISDOM AND LOVE

From the sermon on the day of commemoration for Andrew of Crete

Lord!
In us, there is so much insanity, idiocy, and narrow-mindedness,
But You have all wisdom and love!
Give us just a spark of Your wisdom and love,
Which have been sealed in Your word.
Amen.

I LOVE YOU, LORD

I love You, Lord.
I love You more than anything in the world,
For You are true joy, O my soul.
For Your sake, I love my neighbor as myself.
Amen.

PRAYER BEFORE CONFESSION

Lord, you are our first and last Love.
You are the One for Whom and in Whom we live,
The One we pursue,
And the One by Whom we breathe!

Forgive us that, although we are believers, our faith is so small;
Forgive us that, although we are people who pray, our prayer is
    so weak!
Forgive us that we so infrequently encounter You in true prayer,
And that the words we direct to You become lifeless babble.

Forgive us, Lord, that we are so distracted when we stand before
    an icon,
Open a prayer book, open the Holy Scriptures,
And even when we prepare to partake of the Holy Mysteries.

Forgive us that our lazy, despairing, and tired thoughts wander.
We are guilty before You,
For we are often at church for common prayer only with our feet,
But our lifeless and cold hearts remain somewhere far away.
Amen.

PRAYER BEFORE COMMUNION

✦ Lord! You see that I have broken Your will every day of my life.
I did not just leave like the Prodigal Son; I rebelled against You.
I became your enemy in all my thoughts, deeds, and emotions.
Can you forgive me, Lord? Will you allow me into your Holy
   Place?
For this I ask and pray.

Forgive all that I have forgotten.
Lord, heal me and cleanse me from all I have done out of
   ignorance or misunderstanding.
Heal me from the many sins I have committed from my
   childhood and youth,
Sins that plague me like ulcers.

Lord Jesus Christ,
Allow me to approach this Holy Cup and be joined with the
   bonds of love
That the Holy Church is giving me today, here and now.

Lord, You Yourself said,
"Where two or three are gathered together in My name,
I am there in the midst of them."
Send down your Holy Spirit on all of us gathered here.
Illumine us with Your blessing and make us Your children.

Lord, we stand before You, having examined our lives.
We have all transgressed and broken Your commands.
Our baptismal robe bears all the dirty stains of our unworthy,
   unchristian, and pagan lives.
Lord, forgive us!
May we be robed in pure clothing, so that we may participate in
   Your Divine Banquet.

Lord Jesus Christ, remove from our hearts the black mark of sin,
And give us the seal of Your Spirit,
That we may return to You,
That we may again find love for You,
And that we may again be transformed from worthless slaves into Your children.

Lord, do not judge us according to our deeds, but according to Your mercy.
Do not judge us according to the law or justice, but according to Your grace.
Forgive, wash, purify, and make what was as if it never were.
Set within our will the firm desire to live a Christian life.
May there be no evil on our lips and no darkness in our thoughts,
And may goodness fill our hearts!

Lord, you are our First and our Last.
You are our One and Only, and we come to you.
But we are afraid and ashamed,
Because we come to You in pride and conceit, in despair and irritation,
Full of silly, vain, and empty thoughts of petty vainglory, vengeance, and envy.
We come, having broken all Your commandments and all Your requests.

"Lord, we are unworthy for You to enter into our house."
Yet all the same, we wait for You and ask You to come.
All the same, we know that Your love overcomes our sinfulness
And that Your blood washes away our imperfection.
We believe, Lord, that You are here with us today and that You join us together;

Cleanse us and set us free.

Let us feel the power of the beating of Your loving heart that is open to us.

Teach us to open the door of our hearts to allow You to come in as a guest in our house.

May we touch You and be inspired by You! May we leave this place as if on wings.

May we know that You are with us,

That You bless us, love us, and heal us,

And that You save us by Your blood and Your heart, and through Your sufferings.

Lord, accept us and bring us to life. Give us Your love that resurrects us.

Lord, may your power be in us.

May You be our true Lord and Master!

Amen.

CHAPTER FOURTEEN

SPIRITUAL GUIDANCE ON PRAYER
SELECTED SERMONS AND LECTURES

✪ SELFLESS PRAYER ✪

Excerpt from a Paschal sermon during the Week of Mary of Egypt
(sixth week of Great Lent)

. . . Each of us knows that when we do not have any particular needs and when everything is calm, our prayer begins to cool. It barely flickers, and we must force ourselves to stand in prayer. Conversely, we quickly turn to prayer in desperate situations, in sickness, in difficulties, and in trials. As the saying goes, when thunder crashes, only then will a man cross himself. Thus, it seems that only *need* awakens us to prayer. So if we were prosperous and if the Lord were to give us all the gifts about which people usually dream—health, success, and prosperity in family life and in work— would we then not even begin to pray? Having thanked Him coldly and distractedly, would we then quickly forget about it? Yes, such things do happen, and we know this from our own bitter experience.

Yet, an oft-repeated psalm says, "The LORD is my light and my Salvation; whom shall I fear?" (Ps. 27:1). This is said about people who sought the Lord Himself, because they needed nothing on this earth. The most important thing is to "love the LORD your God with all your heart, with all your soul, and with all your strength" [Deut. 6:5]. "Seek My face," says the Lord through the psalmist (Ps. 27:8). He means, "Seek not only the gifts that I give you, but seek Me, Myself." Love for Christ is the foundation of our spiritual life. If we do not have this love, then we will be like pagans who approach their gods in order to receive some immediate need from them.

Our prayer must be purified of self-interest. We should ask as a child asks of his mother—just like that, for a child loves his mother. A child does not only reach out to the hand that bears gifts or fulfills needs. A child reaches out for his own mother, because she loves him and because he loves the one who gave birth to him and carried him in her arms. Our prayer must be like this! Not only do we see the generous hand of God and reach out for it, but we also see the Lord Himself, who must always be before us, as if crucified before our very eyes.

Amen.

❧ PRAYING FOR OUR NEIGHBORS ❧

Excerpt from a Paschal sermon for the week of Gregory Palamas

. . . Daily prayer for one another should not just be a listing of names. Here in church, we read off names, because we often do not know the people for whom you have requested prayer. But when you yourselves pray for your neighbors, friends, and relatives, as well as for those in need, pray genuinely with the same persistence that the relatives or friends of the paralytic demonstrated when they attempted to get him into the house where the Lord was teaching (Mk. 2:3–5, Lk. 5:18–20). . . .

Only the pursuit of the Lord and the desire to touch Christ the Healer can provide victory. We are currently in the midst of a fast, so we are trying to pray more and to exert more self-control. To abstain from food is not enough, for it is a tiny, microscopic sacrifice to God. Let us try to take heart and offer prayers to the Lord. And this time, let us pray for one another, not for ourselves, not for our health, success, prosperity, or salvation, but for our sisters and brothers, for those who are precious to our heart.

Bring your prayers for them to the Lord today, as the gospel teaches. Pray that their ways would be blessed and that the Lord would support them and meet them where they are. Then, as if our hands were joined together by this prayer and by love, we will all ascend higher and higher to the Lord. This is the main thing, the most significant thing in our life, and everything else will fall into place.[107] And then, Jesus, seeing our faith, will say to all of us and to those for whom we have been praying, "Child, awaken from your sleep and illness, from weakness and spiritual paralysis. Stand. Your sins are forgiven." Amen.

☾ ON THE JESUS PRAYER ☽

Excerpt from a lecture called "Christianity"
at the Moscow House of Machinery, on September 8, 1990
(the day before Father Alexander was murdered)

An abyss lies between the Creator and creation, like that between the absolute and the conditional. This abyss can be jumped neither by logic nor by earthly means. Yet there is a *bridge* that spans the entire abyss. Even the Apostle Paul perceived this bridge, for he saw Christ and internally united himself with Him. He was bound to Christ with endless love in such a way that he felt as if he carried Christ's wounds on himself and that he had died with Christ on the cross and was resurrected with Him. As he said: "It is no longer I who live, but Christ lives in me," and "if we died with Christ, we believe that we shall also live with Him" (Gal. 2:20; Rom. 6:8).

If we cannot be united with God, then we can be united with the God-Man (Christ), for He belongs simultaneously to two worlds: ours and the one beyond. The entire journey of Christian mystics is built upon this, from Paul to today. The way to the Father is only through the Son. "I am the door," said Christ (John 10:9). He is the door, the gate to heaven.

By repeating various prayers, Christian ascetics may be compared to Hindu ascetics who repeat different mantras. In this comparison, there are similarities and parallels. But one of the main prayers in Christian asceticism is called "the Jesus Prayer." In this prayer, one name is constantly repeated—the name of the only begotten One, the One who lived in this world, the Crucified One, the Resurrected One.

This Christocentric aspect of the chief Christian prayer radically differentiates it from all other forms of meditation or mantra, because here there is *an encounter*. This is not just concentrated thoughts or staying focused. It is not just immersion into some ocean or abyss of spirituality, but it is an encounter of an individual with the person of Jesus Christ, Who stands over the world and in the world.

This reminds me of one of Ivan Turgenev's *Poems in Prose*. In his poem "Christ," the narrator stands in a country church and suddenly feels that Christ is standing next to him. Upon turning around, he sees just another person. But when he turns back, he again feels that Christ is there. It's true. That's how it is. The Church of Christ exists and grows, because Christ stands within it, and within each of us.

⊛ ON THE EUCHARIST ⊛

Excerpt from the lecture "Divine Worship as a Synthesis of the Arts," delivered at the Krasnaya Presnya Club in Moscow on December 19, 1989

We call our main service the Eucharist, which means thanksgiving. *Thanksgiving* is a sacred word, and anyone with an honorable soul cannot help but sense this. One French writer, an atheist, said shortly before dying, "I lived a wonderful life. I don't know who to thank for it, but I give thanks with my whole heart."

We Christians thank God. The most noble and exalted prayer takes place when a person full of great emotion understands how very undeserving he is to have received the amazing gift of life, love, friendship, beauty, work, and the mind—all that makes life rich and wonderful. We even thank God for the gift of life's trials and difficulties, because they genuinely temper a strong soul. Remember Pushkin's expression, "As a heavy hammer smashes glass, so does it forge steel." So we should be thankful for everything, but first of all, for the eternal, the inconceivable, and the immeasurable that has entered into our life.

❦ ON INNER SILENCE ❧

Excerpt from a Paschal sermon on the week of Gregory Palamas[108]

In the name of the Father, and of the Son, and of the Holy Spirit!

The Church dedicates the second Sunday of Great Lent to Saint Gregory Palamas, the patron saint of Christian monks who have taken a vow of silence and prayer, those ascetics who in the days of old were called the silent ones (*hesychasts*). They tried to maintain silence in their hearts, while hidden in the reclusive cells of Mount Athos, which is cut off from the whole world by cliffs and the sea. To this day, many monks still live in the same caves where the early *hesychasts* lived. Why do we specifically glorify this saint, the protector of *hesychasts*, during Great Lent? We do so, because at this time it is critical for us to learn and to remind ourselves about silence and *hesychasm*.

What is our life like? It is filled with noise and commotion. The entire existence of modern man is accompanied by numerous sounds of the life around us. A person, especially one living in the city, constantly hears noises such as the revving of automobiles and bustling crowds. . . . Doctors say this affects our health, but let us consider something else. First and foremost, this noise disperses our soul's focus. Many of us, when we find ourselves in a moment of silence, already feel awkward and anxious. We are not at all accustomed to silence, and when we are with others, we cannot keep quiet. And how many superfluous words! . . .

All of this chaos and commotion that consumes our life does not allow us to turn within and remember what is most important. This situation continues until our very last breath. . . . Sometimes, sickness abruptly interrupts our fast pace and lands us in bed, and we suddenly find ourselves torn from the common rat race. At these times, we have a chance to be alone with ourselves. In such minutes, we begin to think, "For what have I been living? Toward what have I been running? Why have I been in such a hurry?" . . .

God's voice always resounds in the silence. If you want to hear it, try to set aside at least a few moments out of the day. For this purpose, the Church gives us the prayer rule: a few minutes to read prayers, to come to yourself, and to consider how the past day went and how the next day will go. This is important. In fact, it is critical.

Whoever wants to know the will of God should seek silence. Whoever wants to collect his thoughts and emotions should seek silence, because our thoughts and emotions are scattered and do not submit to us. We live in constant confusion, but the true spiritual life is achieved only when a person is composed and is in inner unity. We must each gather our thoughts and emotions into the quiet abode in the depths of our hearts, so that silence could reside there—a silence in which God will speak His word to us. If we will not force and compel ourselves to be silent, and if we remain under the power of worldly noise and the endless race, then our whole lives will occur on the surface, with no depth and no spirituality, and without ever really encountering the Lord.

That is the reason we are reminded today of the silent monks. That is why the Church calls us today to struggle against empty and useless words, against idle chatter, and against the utilization of the gift of language[109] to our own detriment. The Holy Scriptures tell us, "Set a guard, O LORD, over my mouth; keep watch over the door of my lips" (Ps. 141:3). We ask this of the Lord, but He expects us to take an active part and to desire and receive God's gift—silence in the stillness of His blessing.

Amen.

NOTES FROM THE TRANSLATOR AND EDITOR

I T HAS BEEN AN HONOR TO TRANSLATE AND EDIT THIS WORK by Father Alexander Men. We have each been challenged in our own prayer lives, and we look forward to utilizing this book as a practical reference for years to come. Christa was the primary translator, but she and April worked as a team to refine the translations for an English-speaking audience.

On occasion, we have transliterated Russian words within the text or endnotes and have shown them in *italics*. When we have done so, we have followed the transliteration system of the Library of Congress within the endnotes. In the text, however, we have deviated slightly from the Library of Congress system. First, we have utilized the common English spellings of such names as Tolstoy (instead of Tolstoi) and Alexander (instead of Aleksandr). Second, the word *I* is transliterated as *"Ya"*, rather than *"Ia"* (see below for this term's usage). Finally, we have not used diacritical marks, including the one at the end of the author's last name (usually transliterated *Men'*). For the pronunciation of Father Alexander's last name, keep in mind that the *e* in Russian is pronounced "ye," but with the soft sign at the end of his name, the vowel resembles a breathy "yay."

Father Alexander periodically uses the term *"I"* (*"Ya"*) in quotation marks as a third-person subject. This terminology is commonly used in Russian religious philosophy and signifies a person's innermost being and truest self. In this book, we have considered the context to translate each use of *"I"* with the best possible English word. Frequently, this translation is "your 'You.'" To indicate each usage, we follow the translated word or phrase with a parenthetical notation (*"Ya"*).

We have attempted to maintain ecumenical language. For example, Father Alexander uses the Orthodox practice of calling a prayer by its first few words. We have, however, often translated his "Our Father" as "the Lord's Prayer." In addition, the Orthodox terminology for *Mysteries* can advisedly be used interchangeably with *sacraments*. We have utilized the terminology *sacraments*, where appropriate, for the benefit of Western readers.

Father Alexander used many standard practices for Russian writers, including the use of the pronoun *him* to refer to any person. We have retained this usage, but the reader should understand that Father Alexander is addressing all believers, not just males. In addition, it is common for Russian authors to write in very short paragraphs. We have often combined many of these into larger paragraphs, where it has made sense to do so. We have also maintained the original italics used by Father Alexander, except where it seemed unusual to do so for an English-speaking audience.

We have changed the order of the original contents of the second Russian edition in three ways. First, we moved chapter two, chapter ten, and chapter thirteen to their current locations for thematic coherence. Second, we have not included the full *Handbook for the Orthodox Christian* as a separate chapter, due to its highly specific historical context; it was written for new Orthodox believers in the Soviet Union, and much of it was so specific to this context that it would not have been appropriate for a twenty-first-century, English-speaking audience. Parts of this handbook that pertain to common practice and to prayer have been included in Appendix B. Finally, we have not included all of the sermons that were in the second edition, because much of Father Alexander's *Paschal* sermon series has already been translated into English (*Awake to Life!* [Torrance, CA: Oakwood Publications, 1996]). Thus, Chapters Twelve and Fourteen offer selected sermons and lectures, most of which have not already appeared in English translation.

In Part II, Father Alexander cites several authors. Many of the sources he cites were either pre-revolutionary books or self-published, typed manuscripts passed around in the late Soviet period (called *samizdat*) and yet not officially published (due to the censorship on religious literature during the Soviet era). At times, the editors of the original Russian text had trouble locating the sources being cited. We were able to locate many of them, and wherever possible, we also located a source that had already been translated into English. In these instances, we cite the English source, rather than the Russian one; with few exceptions, we have provided these sources' English translations within the text. Original endnotes by Father Alexander or the editors of the Russian edition are in [brackets]; we have supplied all others for historical, linguistic, or liturgical clarification.

ACKNOWLEDGMENTS

W E WOULD FIRST LIKE TO THANK PAVEL VOLFOVICH MEN and Natalia Fiodorovna Grigorenko of The Alexander Men Foundation (Russia) for the permission to translate and publish this work for an English-speaking audience. Since Father Alexander's death, his brother Pavel and his wife Natalia have worked tirelessly through the Foundation to preserve, promote, and publish his work.

Thanks also to Gentry Anderson, Steve Henne, Bronwyn McLellan, and Stephen Ullstrom for reading through the first nine chapters and offering their initial thoughts concerning the translation. Special thanks go to the staff at Paraclete Press for guiding this book to its final publication. We are especially grateful to Jon Sweeney, the Publisher, for his encouragement and helpful advice.

April would like to acknowledge her indebtedness to Lil Copan for suggesting the idea of translating one of Father Alexander's books and extending the invitation to take on the project. Thanks also to Christa for her excellent translation work and for becoming a friend over the process of compiling the manuscript. I am grateful to my family and friends for their support and patience during the many months of my work on this project—especially to Nathan and Bronwyn McLellan, Eric and Gentry Anderson, Jan Therkildsen, and Larry and Toni French. Many thanks also to the Laburnum Street community in Vancouver (Regent College) and to my church families, First Baptist Church (Powell, WY), Holy Trinity Anglican Church (Vancouver, BC), and All Saints Episcopal Church (Belmont, MA).

Christa sends heartfelt thanks to all of her friends and family who prayed for her and the translation of this book. Special thanks to April for giving me this wonderful experience, to Jennifer Jannakos for the hours she put into helping me, and to my husband Alexey who tirelessly answered all of my questions about the original Russian text. Thank you to my loving and supportive home parish, All Saints of North America (Albuquerque, NM), for your excitement and encouragement throughout this process.

Finally, we would like to dedicate this work to the everlasting memory of Father Alexander Men who, through his words and deep devotion, has continued to encourage and strengthen us and our wider communities in our journey of prayer.

EXERCISES TO ENHANCE FOCUSED PRAYER

This section first appeared as the appendix to the original version of Father Alexander's A Practical Guide to Prayer. *Although these exercises are not typical for a book on prayer, it was Father Alexander's intention that they be included to help facilitate his readers' practice in regular prayer.* [110]

I. BREATHING

Most people breathe poorly. Their lungs are never fully ventilated. With each breath, people use only a small part of the lungs' 70 million alveoli. Because of this, people suffer physically, in their nervous system, and in their psychological balance. Consequently, their prayer also suffers. It is necessary for a person to learn to breathe well, both for biological balance and for prayer.

You need not put too much emphasis on technical methods, but you should not ignore them either. They are among the beneficial factors that help with concentration. The experience of many centuries, accumulated in a wide variety of religions, confirms their benefit.

A Lesson in Breathing

To learn to breathe is to expand lung capacity by exercising various muscles and allowing the lungs to expand on different levels. There are three distinct levels, depending on the muscles used for breathing.

1. The foundational level is diaphragm breath, or breathing with the diaphragm and belly. It is at this level of breathing that the most air is pulled into the lungs.

2. The second level is chest-breathing, based upon one's air capacity.

3. Finally, the work of the muscles of the upper rib cage leads to the largest expansion of the upper part of the chest cavity and brings forth something called clavicular breath.

Special Exercises

A. *Initial Advice:* It is best to practice your breathing outside in the fresh air or in a well-ventilated room. Your clothing should not be tight. Always breathe through your nose (at the beginning, however, you may breathe through your mouth for increased control in the exhale). Start by exhaling. The exhale, as a rule, should take twice as long as the inhale. Try to develop breathing through the belly (diaphragm breathing), which is the most important and the most often neglected.

The beginning exercise I suggest here is safe for healthy individuals. This may not be true for some exercises on breath control that are suggested in a series of modern works on this subject. You should only perform such exercises under the supervision of a competent instructor.

B. *Exercises:* Lie on your back. Place one hand on your belly (with your elbow on the floor to alleviate tension). Place your other hand on the side of your chest to control the movement of your breathing. Bend your knees, keeping the bottoms of your feet flat on the floor. Your spine should be straight, with your head in a natural position.

Begin by feeling your breath in the way we have already discussed above. Little by little, perceive what is "breathing" in you, and allow yourself to be lulled by your breath. Feel how your breath opens the lungs' alveoli and flows through your organs. Then push your breath out. Exhale slowly, regularly, and quietly. Feel how your diaphragm ascends into your chest cavity. Expel all your air. Feel how your belly falls and your ribs move together. Take a brief pause for one second when your lungs are empty.

Then inhale slowly (it may be more accurate to say that you should allow your lungs to be filled with air on their own). Feel how your belly is filled. Take a brief pause with full lungs (never force it!). Then exhale again.

There is no need to tighten or tense up, or to get disappointed if you do not achieve the expected result immediately. Do three or four full cycles of breathing in this manner, then allow your breathing to return to its natural rhythm.

Exercises throughout the Day

The special exercises described above can be successfully done throughout the day in any position and in any place, unless the air quality is very poor. Breathing exercises should be done without fail any time your attention wanes, when you feel frustration or nervousness, or before a difficult task. Like a pearl diver, inhale and exhale fully before "diving" into your tasks. Besides these few exercises, give your lungs over to their natural movement, not interrupting your breathing with excess attention.

II. COMBATING TENSION (napriazhenie)

What exactly is tension? We discover this gradually when we examine (a) normal and abnormal tension, (b) circumstantial and habitual tension, and (c) levels of tension.

Normal and Abnormal Tension

Normal tension consists of a natural effort that corresponds to a particular physical, mental, moral, or spiritual action. This type of tension is discussed in the section below on relaxation. Abnormal tension occurs when one's effort is extreme and when excessive energy is expended in order to obtain a certain good thing (the achievement of professional success, material prosperity, glory, knowledge, or moral or spiritual perfection) or in order to remove some sort of evil. This abnormal tension is what we need to combat. Here, we will just call it "tension."

Circumstantial and Habitual Tension

Sometimes, a circumstance requires great effort on our part to act and react. When it is necessary to work overtime, to overcome obstacles, or to perform any other difficult task, we need to conserve energy, to properly apportion our efforts, and to choose brief moments in order to pause and disengage. As long as this overexertion is circumstantial, it is harmless. Once it becomes a habit, we need to sound the alarm. We should then realize and understand that this is not normal and that we must do what we can to free ourselves. At the very least, we should turn to relaxation exercises.

Levels of Tension

Regardless of whether our tension is dictated by circumstances or is fully dependent upon us (circumstantial or habitual), we must try to determine at which level of our being the cause and expression of this tension is being experienced.

Physical tension is expressed simultaneously in the muscular and the nervous systems. It manifests itself in the extreme and sometimes overly excessive contraction of certain groups of muscles. More often than not, this affects the muscles of the jaw, the neck, the shoulders, or the fingers. Sometimes nervous tics arise. This tension may be the result of physical labor that is too intense or too long, or of certain life conditions that may or may not be within our control: crowded public transportation, noises, irregular diet, poor air quality, stimulants, or lack of sleep. Usually, physical tension and the resulting fatigue are intensified by these things (unless they occur as a result of another form of tension [i.e., they could just be symptoms of something else]).

Emotional tension. Emotionality, or the realm of the feelings, has varying levels of richness and expression in different individuals. For everyone, this is an area that generates all kinds of tension. Tension may be positive (desiring beauty or searching for love) or negative (worry, depression, or fear). It often hides "underground" by way of suppressed or subconscious complexes. It can be provoked by external circumstances (e.g., the death of a loved one or hardships in life) or by difficult relationships with those close to us (e.g., a tyrannical father or a rude husband). These reasons are often out of our control. We need to attempt at least to balance the affective realm with methods of relaxation and to submit this realm to our spiritual life. If our emotional tension affects our nervous system, physical relaxation and calming the nerves can ease it.

Mental tension. The mental realm is the area of the imagination, memory, and intellect. In this area, tension comes in the form of recurring images, memories, or obtrusive ideas. Tension can arise through an insatiable demand for knowledge, the necessity to study hard, and the exhaustion to which this often leads. It goes without saying that mental tension can often arise for emotional reasons that incite and facilitate obtrusive images and memories.

Spiritual tension is more widely spread than people usually assume. This tension frequently lies behind all other tensions. It often takes on the form of an all-consuming pursuit of mystical enlightenment. Does this not contain a conviction, however subconscious, that perfection is the result of this conquest? Sometimes this tension is generated by a restless demand to have a good opinion about oneself and to have a clean conscience. These moral and spiritual tensions require a moral and spiritual cure. Relaxation exercises can indirectly contribute to this cure.

Moral tension can be called a "passion" for self-perfection and for reaching an ideal. This is the unrestrained desire to succeed in the moral sphere by one's own strength and at any cost. It is expressed by a restless concern not to break any rules and to quickly reach perfection in all virtues. Since this is impossible, a person with such a passion risks developing a compulsive twinge of conscience and its accompanying tension.

Since the various spheres of a person are connected to one another, tensions in different levels project onto one another and mutually amplify one another. The term *tension* is consequently to be understood as a varied and complex phenomenon. Each person must assess for himself: Am I tense? What kind of tensions are these? How are they appearing and being expressed?

RELAXATION EXERCISES

Abnormal tension is the opposite of relaxation, which includes controlled tension. Relaxation is both an important element of a healthy life rhythm and a means to attain the proper rhythm.

Rhythm: Tension and Relaxation

In every well-regulated life, there is an alternation between tension and release, fatigue and rest. This leads to a healthy tiredness that is naturally relieved by relaxation. One can express this rhythm in the form of a sine wave, the end points of which represent tension and relaxation. Excessive but temporary tension can disrupt this rhythm for a moment, but it is quickly restored under the influence of compensating mechanisms that create proportionate relaxation.

As soon as abnormal tension solidly takes hold, this harmonious rhythm can be seriously disturbed for a long time. This leads to a habit of overexertion and to a loss of control. At this point, both activity and relaxation suffer. In order to maintain efforts on this level, one must expend strength in excess of what is available and must use up much nervous energy. In addition, a person becomes incapable of relaxing, thereby cutting off the source for the restoration of nervous energy. This disturbed rhythm can be likened to the groove formed by a saw's teeth, where the upper and lower points gradually grow farther and farther apart. In the final analysis, a person can fall into a pathological cycle of excitation and depression.

The ability to relax eliminates the consequences of abnormal tensions, removes the danger of them becoming permanent, and ensures a flexible way of life, while preserving the harmonious rhythm of exertion and rest. When living in this rhythm, no more is spent than is on hand, and what is spent is restored.

Relaxation as a Method

There are several ways to decrease tension. The term *relaxation*, which is often used incorrectly nowadays, is actually a particular therapeutic method used to treat harmful tension. But we will be speaking of a more general form of relaxation, which is helpful and available to everyone.

First of all, you must determine the reasons for the tension. Are they hidden in either physical or mental overexertion, in all-too-frequent and overly tense emotions, or in unduly impatient quests for the ideal? If so, you should remove those reasons, if at all possible. You may need to say no to a certain activity or put it off for a time. You may need to stop reading certain material or going to certain theatrical productions. Or you may need to throw out certain memories that cause alarm. If this is not possible, then, at the very least, you must find another way to reduce their effect.

If you are performing a difficult task, you must take intermittent breaks for relaxation (see below). If anyone in your family is irritating you, you need to look at this person differently and sense why this person is bothered or disappointed. Then, offer your patience as a gift of love to God.

Medication

In cases of tension that lead to insomnia or extensive fatigue, people often run to synthetic medications—downers, sleep aids, tonics, or stimulants. Sometimes these things are truly helpful when they are taken temporarily. In the worst-case scenario, however, taking these things becomes useless and even dangerous. These medications do not, in and of themselves, provide the necessary deep relaxation and real restoration to the nervous system. They are but a means to attain the true medicine—sleep and rest.

Stimulants speed up the expenditure of nervous energy, after which they quickly lead to a fall in energy levels. Tranquilizers are sometimes necessary, but they can also mask the true reasons for fatigue and insomnia. Sleep is one of the most important medications created by nature. An adult should sleep at least eight hours and children even more. Therefore, you should not work too late or stay up too late talking if you must get up early the next morning. Evening sleep is usually more beneficial than morning sleep for most people. If you suffer from insomnia, it is necessary to determine the reasons for it, so that you can get rid of it (e.g., eating an excessively large dinner, particular worries, etc.). You should not try to force yourself to sleep; that type of tension is the best way to prevent sleep. Instead, think of how you need to put yourself into God's hands: "Lord, into Your hands I commit my spirit."

Pausing throughout the Day

We have much more free time than we think. Throughout the day, we have many opportunities to take breaks for just a few moments—as we transition from one task to another, as we go up or down stairs, as we walk to answer the door bell, as we type a letter, etc. We need to use all of these moments for the relief of tension.

Days Off

You should strive to make these days just as full as the days in your workweek. It is good to set aside time to spend with your family, to create something, to take walks, to read, to listen to music, or just to occupy yourself with any task. However, it is important that these various activities differ from your daily work and are not too tiring.

Extended Vacation

Do not break up these days off into too many short increments. It is helpful to change your environment and climate; to make use of the sun, water, and quiet; and to get physical exercise. Water plays a big role in the "renewal" of the body (showers and baths).

During a vacation, those who do not live an active lifestyle should set aside an hour a day for walking. Find your rhythm. Walk in silence (you should have inner silence as well). Observe the landscape. Listen to the birds singing. Take in the smells. In the summer, walk barefoot through the grass or in the water.

Calming Exercises

These exercises can touch various levels of our being. Controlled breathing (see above) is a wonderful way to achieve peace in one's physical body and nerves. Exercises on mental control (see the next section), particularly the exercise of receptivity, are the best rest for the brain. Directly below, I introduce physical exercises, which facilitate rest in the whole person by acting upon the nervous system.

EXERCISES THROUGHOUT THE DAY

a) First, try to locate the tension in your body. Check yourself. Are your shoulders raised? Are your hands tightly clenched? Is your gait uneven? Is your face distorted, your forehead wrinkled, your jaw clenched, etc.? These things point to intense tension. Simply noticing the tension already causes you to relax. Use a minute of rest to do this.

b) Breathe deeply and slowly, either outside or near an open window.

c) Absorb yourself completely in what you are doing at this moment. Be fully conscious of what you are doing, whether walking, going up stairs, etc. It is helpful to really sense a strong smell, listen to a song, gaze at a photograph, etc.

d) Consciously perform your instinctive gestures. Yawn. Stretch. Walk around a bit. Do all of this consciously, completely giving yourself over to these motions.

e) Slow down your daily rhythm. For just a few minutes, without stopping the task at hand, make yourself do it three times slower than usual. As you do this, pay close attention to the sensation in your muscles. With your muscles, you control the output of the energy you put into a task. Try to exert as little energy as possible to hold a glass, grab a pen, etc.

f) Tighten your muscles fully, then completely release them. For example, raise your shoulders as far as you can, then allow them to fall quickly. Tighten your fingers into a fist, then relax them. Contract all the muscles in your face to the fullest extent and in all directions, then relax them. And so on.

g) Feel the weight of your entire body. There really is a lot of it— 110, 130, 175 pounds! Allow this weight to pull down, as if the earth were a great force desiring to pull you down. Indeed, it really does have the full force of gravity. If you are sitting, feel how your weight pushes you onto the chair. Or allow your arms to hang freely along your body, as if 10 or 12 pounds were hanging only by a thread. Or bend over from your waist, allowing both your arms and your head to hang as if detached from the body. Let them hang loosely by their own weight.

h) Let your eyes rest. The eye is a very delicate organ. When the eyes are tired, it especially affects your head. It is helpful to bend over a table from a sitting position, covering your eyes with your palms (not pushing them into the eye sockets) by placing one palm over the other and resting on your forehead. Two minutes of such darkness will remove tension from the eyes. You can do this while listening to music or while transitioning from one task to another.

Do not do all of these exercises at once. You should try one, then another, and choose the ones that are the most helpful. It is important to maintain flexibility and willingness to change, and to watch that you don't get obsessed. Otherwise, this would lead only to a new form of tension. Little by little, a peaceful state will come about spontaneously.

A PEACEFUL STATE *An Exercise*

Initial Advice

This exercise should be done at a time of leisure and calm, but never immediately after eating (wait three hours). It is best to do the exercise in a room that is well ventilated and sufficiently warm (when we are completely relaxed, our body temperature can drop.). Turn the lights down or close your eyes. For a short time, shut yourself off from all forms of outside stimuli. Loosen your clothing (collar, shoes, etc.). Continue the exercise, even if you do not notice any results. Do not relentlessly pursue your goals, since such an obsession is already a form of tension.

The Exercise

Lie on your back with your hands lying freely at your side, palms up. Your palms should be open and your fingers slightly bent. Your feet should be somewhat apart, opening to the outside. Each person needs to find the most comfortable position. If necessary, place a small pillow under your head, knees, or elbows. Take one or two controlled inhales and exhales, and allow your breathing to return to its natural rhythm.

Phase One: The Principle of Perception

Feel your body. Perceive that it is composed of distinct parts.

Phase Two: The Principle of a Metal Spring

Think of your muscles as metal springs that can extend and come back together. Gently contract each group of muscles; then relax them. Begin by contracting the muscles in your legs, gradually moving all the way up to your head. If this is difficult for you, begin with your head muscles and move down through your legs. Move through the muscles of the fingers, feet, calves, knees, hips, pelvis (first the right side, then the left), the neck, face (jaw, cheeks, ears, eyelids, forehead), and scalp. Then, in complete peace and stillness, repeat the exercise with even less tension. Of course, this can only be accomplished by practicing it day in and day out.

Phase Three: The Principle of Gravity

Remaining completely still, feel how your body is becoming heavy. Perceive yourself to be spread out on the floor, as if rooted to the ground or as if you were stuck in dough.

Do not exit too quickly from this state of perfect calm. Blink your eyes a little, inhale more deeply, begin to move your lips and your fingers, allow your hands to rub each other as if you were washing them, and stretch. Only then should you slowly get up.

After some training, such a session will bring about a state of great physical and internal peace. If you need to shorten the exercise, you can limit yourself to one series of controlled inhales and exhales and to Phase Two (without repetition).

III. MENTAL CONTROL

Let us begin with the common occurrence of distraction during prayer. I pray, and my attention is focused on God. I express to Him my faith, love, and praise. I look at my life in light of Him. My "field of consciousness" is occupied with thoughts about God and feelings and aspirations that relate to Him. Ideas, images, worries, and things that are foreign to the "subject" of my prayer then come into this "field." They emanate from various areas—the body, the senses, the emotions, the imagination, etc. Sometimes they even completely push aside and take the place of any thought of God. Rarely does one have enough mental control to stop hindrances from inserting themselves into the field of consciousness.

This mental control is one of the characteristics of your "You" ("*Ya*") that is activated seemingly automatically. Of course, your "You" ("*Ya*") can consciously react to a flood of obstacles and redouble its attention on God. Yet if the mechanism of control is well tuned, it can push aside that which has nothing to do with thoughts about God. "The field of consciousness" sets "guards" at its borders. These guards monitor ideas, images, and feelings that try to cross the border and turn away everything that is unrelated to prayer.

INSUFFICIENT MENTAL CONTROL

Many people exhibit insufficient mental control, thereby poorly exercising the ability to remove obstacles and stop extraneous thoughts from entering the field of consciousness. In this case, obstacles emerge from various zones of our being and flood the poorly guarded territory in order to attract the attention of your "You" ("*Ya*") and then to gain its consent. These obstacles can be memories of past failures, worries about tomorrow, dreams, etc. Even if your "You" ("*Ya*") does not consent to the dispersal of your attention, and your pursuit of God is mostly preserved, your prayer is still quite difficult and your consciousness is clouded.

A deficiency of mental control testifies to a deficiency of control in your whole life—in household activities, in professional work, etc. When you do not have enough control, ideas and images are not as clear, as if the eye of the mind were out of focus. It is difficult to follow a train of thought. When looking at an object, you do not notice its distinctive features. You do not pay enough attention to the task at hand. This lack of attentiveness hurts the function of the memory. You have trouble recalling what you have read. You experience difficulty when you need to describe precisely what you have seen. You are not sure of what you have done. For example, you have to check three times to determine whether you have turned off the gas on the stove or locked the door.

Unclear thoughts and cloudy recollection causes your will to be uncertain and distracted. You do not have confidence in yourself. How can you move through this fog with hopefulness? Thus, you abandon the task to write a letter or to do something else. When you are torn between the many ideas that demand simultaneous or consistent attention, you must exert ten times more energy than the task requires. From this comes an accustomed fatigue, the absence of enthusiasm and persistence, and, therefore, a lack of effectiveness in your activities. Such insufficiencies manifest themselves in the moral and spiritual life; there is not enough strength and persistence, without which there can be no virtue.

Insufficient mental control can eventually lead to serious problems in the nervous system and in the psyche. As a result of a depletion of nervous energy and a weakening of control, a person is subject to delusions, fears, and feelings of guilt. Consequently, physical problems may arise.

Reasons for Insufficient Mental Control

The main reason for weak mental control is a lack of training in attentiveness. Our mental control has a mechanism for filtering, which must be well tuned. This mechanism is developed through training and through the cultivation of attentiveness. There are two aspects to your attentiveness: your "You" ("Ya") (1) focuses on a chosen subject and (2) simultaneously filters out everything else. Training in attentiveness is at the same time the training of your control, which filters out everything that is not the object of your attention. This is why a lack of control can lead to physical and mental fatigue, partly due to overexertion and worry. Such things quickly weaken the spring mechanism of our attention and control, causing it to work poorly. This is especially noticeable in the evening after a tiring day. Common sense advises you to go to bed as soon as possible, but you just cannot bring yourself to do it (in which case, you must force yourself to go to bed).

DEVELOPING MENTAL CONTROL

The ancients had a saying: "Do what you are doing." This is also a rule of the spiritual life. Live in the present moment, because this is where you meet the Lord. Such an abiding in the present moment, without slipping into the past or the future, develops mental control. It requires and develops a keen point of view and a healthy will, and it facilitates an intensity of activity. This is why the first step toward the establishment of mental control is to dedicate yourself fully to the task at the present moment. And this task could include such activities as walking or eating, opening a door, washing your hands— not just working and praying. Then, the control mechanism, which filters out all other things, is activated. We need to filter out obstacles in our everyday activities—just as we need to do in prayer. It is not enough here to simply utilize our "usual" will. It requires constant exercise and never giving in to inner temptations that oppose the filtering out of "parasitic thoughts."

In addition, it is critical that the control mechanism not come up against opponents that are too strong. We have seen that an unsanctioned distraction attempts to come into our field of consciousness and gives rise to "longings" in various areas. For this reason, it is necessary to restrain these longings out of respect for your "You" ("Ya"). This is not to say that we should destroy these longings (since they can contain useful energy), but we should gather them, put them in order, and bring them into submission—whether they are desires of the body, the emotions, the imagination, or the mind. An effective way to put these lower ambitions into their place is to develop a deep urge for God. This is the role of prayer: it welcomes the mental control that allows you to give yourself more fully to God, the Divine "object." Prayer facilitates this control by submitting the lower ambitions of our spirit's desire to God.

"*Be* in what you are doing." This expression signifies that we need to direct the energy of our will to a particular course of action. But we must still possess this energy. And the energy used to focus attention is energy from the nervous system—or more accurately, from the brain. But why do we need to stimulate our will? We must charge it with mental energy like we charge a battery. How? By being conscious of our senses.

Under the influence of elementary feelings, I am constantly experiencing a sense of the outside world. I see a field of poppies and their beautiful red color. I hear the birds singing. I feel various materials against my skin. I sense what is happening in one of my body's organs: the weakening of my muscles or the rhythm of my breath. These various sensations, perceived by the nervous system, are sent to my brain.

I should be conscious of these sensations and allow them to fully unfold. This signifies a cultivation of receptivity. I must give myself over to this receptivity as a clear photographic film. In reality, my film has an imprint of cares, dreams, and thoughts. When I experience a sensation, I must be careful not to immediately turn it into an idea. I am walking down the street, and all other feelings are excluded. I feel only how my feet touch the ground. You could say that all my focus is in my feet.

This is very difficult. I may experience the pure sensation for merely a second. But in this second, I am strengthening my nervous system and allowing my brain to rest. Consequently, I must spend each free moment doing mental exercises in this state of receptivity, rather than mulling over worries or making up plans. It is a great art to be able to pull oneself away from such things for a few moments a day.

The state of receptivity, which renews energy in the nervous system, subsequently allows us to practice prayer and all other activities with diligence. As a person becomes accustomed to receiving sensations, he not only rests and strengthens his nervous system, but he also becomes capable of a spiritual receptivity that opens him up to God's work in the depths of his being. Then, a transition takes place from active prayer, where human activity predominates, to silent prayer, where the activity of God's Spirit predominates.

EXERCISES FOR MENTAL CONTROL
Receptivity

This requires that we consciously, but passively, receive sensations that come from the internal and external feelings.

A. Internal sensations: Sit down. Find the most comfortable position (straight back, feet flat on the ground, hands resting freely on your knees). Close your eyes and feel the weight of your body on the chair, the pressure of the back of the chair against your back, and the contact of your feet with the floor. Then feel each one of your toes individually, one at a time. Feel the right calf, and then the left, and so on, moving upward in this way to the very top of your head. Then feel your breathing without thinking about it. Inhale slowly through your nose and notice how the air passes through, expanding your abdomen, filling your lungs, and moving your rib cage. Slowly exhale through your mouth and notice how the air passes between your half-closed lips. With your eyes closed, lift your right hand slowly, sensing what is happening, then relax it. Lift the left hand, the left leg, and relax them, etc. The entire time, register these sensations passively. While walking, feel the movement of your muscles, the contact with the ground, the rhythm of your breath, and the wind on your face.

B. *External sensations:* Listen to the sounds that reach your ears, without trying to discern them. Open your eyes. Notice shapes and colors without trying to interpret them or to give them a name. Learn to sense the smells around you. While eating, savor the flavor of the food. When touching objects, focus on their shape and quality (hot, cold, soft, rough, smooth). From time to time throughout the day, "take a vacation." Feel the joy of living. Allow various visual, auditory, and tactile sensations to come to you and to enter into you.

Concentration

Close your eyes, and in your mind draw the number *1* before you. Hold the image. Then wipe it away or start to write it smaller and smaller until it disappears. Or watch it move farther and farther away, like the back side of the last train car as it moves away, until it becomes unnoticeable and disappears.

You could also do this with words or with abstract figures (the infinity sign, a punctuation mark, the treble clef) that are initially quite simple and then later more and more complex. Draw them slowly, then erase them immediately or gradually. The choice of subject for mental concentration is based upon individual taste and depends upon each person's personality. You will come to know this with practice.

SELECTIONS FROM *HANDBOOK FOR THE ORTHODOX CHRISTIAN*

The editors of the second Russian edition of A Practical Guide to Prayer *included a chapter with Father Alexander's* Handbook for the Orthodox Christian. *There were so many new believers in his parish that he decided to write a catechetical guide regarding how to conduct oneself during liturgical services and in various periods of the Christian calendar. Much of this handbook, used only in manuscript form by his parishioners, was applicable for a Soviet Orthodox audience, but we have here included the parts that are useful for an English-speaking, ecumenical audience.*

❧ CONFESSION ❧

Confession usually takes place before the Liturgy, while the Hours are being read in the church or during Matins. If there are at least two priests in the church, then confessions may be held through the beginning of the Liturgy. One priest serves, and the other hears confessions. When there are many people in the church, there will be a general confession. In a general confession, the priest reads off sins, and the people repent in their hearts before God. If there is a particular sin weighing on your soul that was not mentioned during the general confession, you should approach the priest to confess this sin after all others have confessed, so you do not delay the process. Remember that you must not limit yourself only to general confessions. You must absolutely augment them with private confessions as well. When you want to confess, you must arrive at church early and stand on the side where confessions will be heard (an analoy will usually already be set up), so that you do not have to walk back and forth across the sanctuary.

Confession consists of the following parts:

1. A prayer by the priest
2. The priest's words to the penitent
3. The confession of sins before the cross and the Gospels that are on the analoy
4. Advice and instructions from the priest and, if he deems it necessary, penance
5. The prayer of absolution

While the priest reads the prayer of absolution, he covers the head of the one confessing (the penitent) with his epitrachilion. The penitent bows his head low. After the prayer, the penitent kisses the

Gospels and the cross. As he does this, he calls to mind that the Law of God, which he has transgressed, is written in the Gospels and that, by the cross of Christ, his sins are wiped away. A priest does not absolve a person of his sins by his own power, but by the power of Christ that was given to the priest in the sacrament of ordination.

The Holy Church compares the work done by a priest at confession with the work of a doctor. We come to the spiritual hospital, and in order not to leave uncured, we must learn to accurately name our sins, so the spiritual doctor can prescribe the correct treatment. You should prepare for confession ahead of time, at home, evaluating your conscience against the Beatitudes. If we hide anything during confession, we do not sin against the priest (who is just a man), but against Christ Himself. In such a case, the absolution given by the priest and the Communion itself are "unto judgment and condemnation."[111]

When we, having overcome our shame and humiliation, confess our sins to our spiritual leader, we have performed a small "feat," without which a sincere confession remains incomplete. The person who has confessed must beware of thoughts that claim that he will lose face in the eyes of the priest if he tells him of his sinful deeds and thoughts. This ensnaring thought hinders authentic confession. Remember that the grace of ordination allows the priest not to lose his rapport with the penitent, even if he has committed a grave sin. Confession and a conversation with a priest outside of confession are two different types of fellowship. Outside of confession, a priest can speak simply as a person, a friend, or a helper. Before the cross and the Gospels, he is performing a sacrament.

☾ COMMUNION ☽

A person who rarely takes Communion is doing a great disservice to his own spiritual life. The Holy Fathers called Christians to take Communion every time they attended Liturgy.[112] Even if we have moved away from this practice in modern times, it is still good to take Communion at least once every forty days and without fail on your saint's day. Saint Seraphim of Sarov told us to come to Communion no less than 16 times per year.

On the night before taking Communion, people observe a fast and read "Prayers in Preparation for Communion" from the prayer book (see also Chapter Thirteen). On the morning before Communion, people do not eat or drink anything until the Liturgy is over. This is out of reverence for the Holy Feast of Communion. Those who smoke must abstain from smoking. People come to the Holy Cup only after confession. Confession and Communion are two separate sacraments. The practice of the Russian Orthodox Church ties them closely together for the simple reason that we should not come to the Holy Cup without first reconciling with God through the sacrament of confession. Sometimes, if a person is not prepared for Communion, he may come only to confession.

Communion takes place toward the end of the Liturgy, after we have sung "Our Father" and immediately after the Communion hymn. When the Cup is brought out, we say the prayer "I believe, O Lord, and I confess" to ourselves, along with the priest. Then we approach the Holy Cup in silence and reverence, crossing our arms across our chest right over left. We do not cross ourselves in front of the Cup. We tell the priest the full name given to us at baptism. After receiving the Holy Mysteries, we kiss the bottom edge of the Cup and proceed to the table where we receive a sip of warm wine or juice and a piece of the *prosphora*. This symbolizes the agape feasts of the earliest Christians.[113]

⊚ ORTHODOX FASTS ⊚

In our human nature, the harmony between the spirit and the flesh has been destroyed. The flesh strives to rule over the spirit. Any person living a spiritual life must, therefore, use at least the most basic forms of *askesis* (self-denial). One of these methods is fasting. Abstaining from animal products is significant in two ways. Fasting reins in the nature of the flesh and develops a person's will and fortitude through obedience to the Church. Christ Himself blessed the act of fasting. He showed his disciples the necessity of abstinence by the example of His fasting.

The various levels of fasting can be roughly characterized by the following categories:

Very strict fast (*xerophagy*, or "dry eating"). Eat only raw plant food with no oil.

Strict fast. Eat all types of cooked fruits and vegetables with vegetable oil.

Standard fast. Add fish to the strict fast.

Relaxed fast. The infirm, travelers, and those who eat in a cafeteria may eat everything except meat.

The Church allows the cancellation or relaxation of a fast under certain circumstances (illness, traveling, etc.). However, a Christian *should not cancel or relax the fast on his own (nor should he make it stricter), but he should ask for a blessing from his spiritual director.*

Fasting is not just a time of physical abstinence. It is also a time of greater battle against sin, of particular concentration in prayer, and of more frequent communion. There are four extended fasts in the year. In addition to these, the Church has appointed Wednesdays and

Fridays as days of fasting throughout the entire year. In memory of certain events, there are other one-day fasts.

EXTENDED FASTS

Great Lent occurs before *Pascha* (Easter) and lasts for a total of seven weeks. This is a *strict* fast. The *very strict* weeks of fasting are the first, the fourth (the Week of the Veneration of the Cross), and the seventh (Passion Week, or Holy Week). The fast ends during Passion Week after Liturgy on Holy Saturday, but traditionally, most people do not break the fast until after the *Paschal* Liturgy, which is the night before Holy Pascha. Great Lent is part of the Paschal Cycle and therefore falls on different dates in different years depending on the date of the celebration of *Pascha*.[114]

Saint Peter's Fast (known in America as the Fast of Peter and Paul or the Apostles' Fast) occurs before the Feast of the Holy Apostles Peter and Paul (June 29). It begins on the Monday after the feast day of All Saints (the Sunday after Pentecost) and continues until June 29. This fast changes in length each year depending on the celebration of *Pascha*. This is a *standard* fast, not as strict as the others.

The Dormition Fast occurs before the Feast of the Dormition (Assumption) of the Mother of God. It always falls on the same dates: August 1–15. This is a *strict* fast.

The Nativity Fast (Advent, sometimes called Saint Philip's Fast) begins on the day after the Feast of the Apostle Philip. It is always on the same dates: November 15 to December 25. This is a *strict* fast on weekdays, and a *standard* fast on Saturdays and Sundays.

ONE-DAY FASTS

Wednesdays and Fridays are *standard* fast days throughout the entire year, except for Bright Week (the week following *Pascha*) and the Fast-

Free Weeks (the period from Nativity to Theophany Eve [December 25 to January 4], the week following the Sunday of the Publican and the Pharisee, and Trinity Week [the week following Pentecost]).

The Baptism Fast is a *very strict* fast held on January 5, the day before Theophany (Epiphany). In Russia, there is a folk tradition not to eat anything until sundown on this day.

The Beheading of John the Baptist is a *strict* fast on August 25.

The Elevation of the Precious Cross of our Lord is a *strict* fast on September 14.

EXAMINATION OF CONSCIENCE[115]

Father Makarii of Optina said he had insight into hearing confessions and dealing with people through inner knowledge. Father Alexander Men would say this is how he prepared the examination of conscience for general confession, by knowing his own heart, so people would feel that he was speaking directly to them. Outside of confession, in everyday relations, he had that quality of being with people so attentively that each would feel as if he were their unique friend.

Bishop Seraphim (Sigrist)[116]

☽ EXAMINATION OF CONSCIENCE ☾

The text below is just one example of the type of questions Father Alexander would ask his parishioners, to aid in their preparation for confession. One of his parishioners likely recorded (and later transcribed) these questions one time as he spoke them.

1. What has your general emotional "tone" been recently (or the "backdrop" of the last six months or so)? Has it been predominantly bright, dark, or fluctuating? Are there any new influences that you can connect to this "backdrop"? If you cannot pinpoint them, why? Have you had feelings of inexplicable panic, unclear anxiety, constant discontentment, feelings of weakness, or drained energy? Is any of this at all related to your faith and prayer?

2. What has been dominant: feelings of loss or feelings of gain? Have you had feelings of serious failure or success in life? If something like this is true in your life, ask yourself what exactly you consider (in the depths of your soul) to be success or failure. Is there a personal lesson you can take from this that can be connected to your faith? Can you find a confirmation of your faith in them?

3. Has it ever occurred to you to evaluate your life on the basis of whether you have experienced joy, happiness, and true contentment? Should these exist and is it worth it to expend energy on them? Why? Is your life limited to the opposing ideas of what you want and what is required? If so, why do you so easily give in to the world around you on the basis of your right to joy and happiness, or at least to some "pleasure" in life?

4. In what situations is it most difficult for you to be honest and open about your thoughts, emotions, and feelings? Is this related to some kind of external ideological pressure, to the preaching of the faith, or to something else? Is it difficult for you to be yourself in "normal" situations, when you are not required to justify your basic life decisions? Is it more difficult for you to be around believers or nonbelievers? Why?

5. When it comes to life circumstances, has a sense of inner freedom grown in you? Have you succeeded in minimizing the burden of your circumstances, or have you even tried? Why? Has your faith and prayer helped you in this? Has anything else helped?

6. Is there a life situation, a problem, a person, a group, or an organization that is interfering with your life? Is it stifling, belittling, or challenging you? How do you tend to respond?

Do you accept it, fight it, get angry, get depressed, hate it, or avoid it? Why? Is your reaction related to faith and hope in God or to a sense of self-worth? Do you have a desire to fight and be brave?

7. When you have time to be alone, what are your tendencies? Do you extend or avoid this time? Do you withdraw mentally into your worries about the present? Do you focus on your inner pain? Or do you withdraw into thoughts about the past or dreams for the future? Why? Do you experience peace, agitation, despair, or inspiration during this time? Why? Do you tend to contemplate the events and results in your life in light of your faith? Do you turn to prayer? Or do you have to force yourself to do these things?

8. Do you have a close friend? If yes, what made this friendship possible? If not, why not? Could a church fellowship take that place? Or does the church have another purpose in your life?

9. Make a descriptive portrait of yourself the way you would like to see yourself and of your friends the way you would like to see them. Why did you portray yourself and your friends this way? Now make a second portrait of how you see your life, yourself, and your friends as they are currently. How do these portraits differ? Why? Should these differences be removed? Why and in what way?

10. Are there often tasks in your life that you would like to begin with prayer? Why do you think that is?

11. Is your main life calling clear to you? How would you express it if someone asked about it? Are you succeeding in bringing it to fruition? Why? What is hindering you? If Jesus were to ask you directly what you were to consider to be the main result of your life at this time, would you have anything to say?

12. Have you ever been able to commit an act on the basis of truly unconditional love? Why or why not? What spiritual lesson has brought you success (or failure) in acts of love? What significance did you ascribe to this?

13. Have you ever had to truly forgive anyone of anything? Is there anyone or anything that you cannot forgive? Why not?

14. When you have seriously and sincerely answered all of the above questions, then you can ask yourself the following questions: Is there a real sense in your life of God's personal presence and personal intervention in your daily activities and in your destiny? Do you expect His love and attention or, "out of modesty," do you not expect very much? Have you experienced the Lord's call personally directed to you? Has he revealed Himself in any way? Have you been "touched" by the Holy Spirit recently? Were you ready and willing to respond? What responsive step have you taken recently? Heeding Jesus and the Holy Spirit, can you honestly say that you have overcome your own resistance [to obey] and the resistance of the world for the sake of love, for the sake of your calling, for the sake of holiness, and for the Lord's sake?

ORTHODOX PRAYERS

A collection of the prayers mentioned by Father Alexander, in order of their appearance in the text.

REJOICE, O VIRGIN!

◆ Rejoice! O Virgin Theotokos!
Mary, full of Grace, the Lord is with you.
Blessed are you among women,
And blessed is the fruit of your womb,
For you have borne the Savior of our souls!

. . .

PRAYER OF SAINT EPHREM OF SYRIA

◆ O Lord and Master of my life,
Take from me the spirit of sloth, despair, lust of power, and
   idle talk.*

But give rather the spirit of chastity, humility, patience, and
   love to Thy servant.*

Yea, O Lord and King,
Grant me to see my own transgressions, and not to judge my
   brother,
For blessed art Thou, unto ages of ages. Amen.*

* prostration

WHAT SWEETNESS OF LIFE

What sweetness of life abides unaccompanied with grief?

What glory stands unchanged upon earth?

All things are but most-feeble shadows;

All things are but most-deluding dreams.

Yet a moment, and death takes all these things.

But in the light of Thy countenance, O Christ,

And in the sweetness of Thy Beauty,

As the Lover of Mankind give rest unto him (her)

Whom Thou hast chosen.

This prayer portion is from the Office for the Burial of a Layman,
which is attributed to Saint John the Monk. The full prayer is
available in The Great Book of Needs *(Volume III).*

TROPARION FOR THE FEAST OF THE NATIVITY OF CHRIST

Thy Nativity, O Christ our God,

Has shone to the world the light of wisdom!

For by it those who worshiped the stars

Were taught by a star to adore Thee,

The Sun of Righteousness,

And to know Thee, the Orient from on high!

O, Lord, glory to Thee!

OPEN TO ME THE DOORS OF REPENTANCE

Open to me the doors of repentance, O Giver of Life;
For my soul rises early to pray toward your holy Temple,
Bearing the temple of my body all defiled.
But in your compassion, purify me
By the loving-kindness of your mercy.

NOTES

Editor's Note: Material within brackets indicates notes that appeared in the Russian edition.

1. *Tamizdat* editions of these works include A. Bogoliubov [Aleksandr Men'], *Syn Chelovecheskii (The Son of Man)* (Brussels: La Vie avec Dieu, 1968); Emmanuil Svetlov [Aleksandr Men'], *V poiskakh Puti, Istiny i Zhizni: Istoriia Religii (In Search of the Way, the Truth, and the Life: The History of Religions)*, 6 vols. (Brussels: La Vie avec Dieu, 1970–1983). All of these works have been republished multiple times in the post-Soviet period. An English translation of *Syn Chelovecheskii* is available: Alexander Men, *Son of Man: The Story of Christ and Christianity*, trans. Samuel Brown (Crestwood, NY: St. Vladimir's Seminary Press, 1998).

2. The three works in the Life in the Church series include *Heaven on Earth* (later entitled *Sacrament, Word and Image; samizdat* 1960, *tamizdat* 1969), *How to Read the Bible* (*samizdat* 1976, *tamizdat* 1981), and *A Practical Guide to Prayer* (*samizdat* late 1970s, published 1991). The latter is the first book of the series to be translated into English as the book you now hold.

3. One section of this second expanded edition, the *Handbook for the Orthodox Christian*, has not been fully translated here, due to its highly specific audience (new and "cradle" Orthodox believers in the Soviet Union who were finding it challenging to worship together). In Appendix B we have included sections from this handbook that are suitable to an ecumenical audience. In addition, several sermons from this second edition have already been translated into English in Fr. Alexander Men, *Awake to Life! Sermons from the Paschal (Easter) Cycle*, foreword by Bishop Seraphim (Sigrist), trans. Marite Sapiets (Torrance, CA: Oakwood Publications, 1996). We have, therefore, omitted them from this translation and have only provided translations of sermons that had not yet been available in English.

4. Certain circles of Orthodox Christians are highly critical of Father Alexander Men for his ecumenism. Some extremists in the Russian Orthodox Church criticize him for being a Jew, while others accuse him of being a heretic. In 1998, Bishop Nikon of Ekaterinburg approved of the burning of books by Fathers Alexander Men, John Meyendorff, and Alexander Schmemann. For an informed, albeit dated, discussion of the controversy surrounding Father Alexander Men, see Michael Plekon, "Alexander Men: A Modern Martyr, Free in the Faith, Open to the World," in *Living Icons: Persons of Faith in the Eastern Church* (Notre Dame, IN: University of Notre Dame Press, 2004), 234–60.

5. The terms *spiritual son, spiritual daughter*, and *spiritual children* are used by and about those to whom Father Alexander ministered and who came under his authority as a spiritual director. In the 1970s and 1980s, he maintained an active correspondence with various spiritual children spread throughout the USSR and recent émigrés to Europe, Israel, and North America.

6. For example, he invited Sister Ioanna (Julia Reitlinger) to "commune" with him in prayer from a distance. Sister Ioanna, in her later years, corresponded extensively with Father Alexander from her "chosen exile" in Central Asia. In 1956, she chose to return to the USSR from Paris, where she had been an émigré iconographer under the spiritual direction of Fr. Sergius Bulgakov. The Soviet state would only allow her to reside in Uzbekistan. Father Alexander, though much younger than Sister Ioanna, became her spiritual director in 1975. See *Umnoe Nebo: Perepiska protoiereia Aleksandra Menia s monakhinei Ioannoi (Iu. N. Reitlinger) (The Wise Sky: The Correspondence of Father Alexander Men with the Nun Ioanna (J. N. Reitlinger))* (Moscow: Fond imeni Aleksandra Menia, 2002).

7. See, for example, the letters reproduced in Zoia Maslenikova, "Moi Dukhovnik" ("My Spiritual Director"), in *Aleksandr Men': Zhizn' (Alexander Men: A Life)*, 2nd ed. (Moscow: Zakharov, 2001), 230, 232.

8. Particularly clear statements of the importance he places on "encounter" include Father Alexander Men, *Awake to Life!*, 49–51; Aleksandr Men', *Istoki Religii (The Origins of Religion)*, vol. 1 of *V Poiskakh Puti, Istiny, i Zhizni*, 3rd ed. (Moscow: EKSMO, 2004), 66–67, 70, 72.

9. Autogenic training is a relaxation technique developed in Germany in the 1930s. It involves three daily practice sessions of around 15 minutes each, during which an individual uses visualization techniques to promote relaxation.

10. The work mentioned here is *Heaven and Earth* by Lord Byron (1788–1824). In the play, one character (a mortal in the flood) makes the following soliloquy: "He gave me life—he taketh but / The breath which is his own: / And though these eyes should be forever shut, / Nor longer this weak voice before his throne / Be heard in supplicating tone, / Still blessed be the Lord, / For what is past, / For that which is: / For all are his, / From first to last— / Time—space—eternity—life—death— / The vast known and immeasurable unknown. / He made, and can unmake; / And shall I, for a little gasp of breath, / Blaspheme and groan? / No; let me die, as I have lived, in faith, / Nor quiver, though the universe may quake!"

11. The Russian expression used here is an idiom, which literally means, "The eyes are afraid; the hands act." We have here translated it to capture the meaning of the Russian idiom in English.

12. The saying to which Father Alexander is referring was actually an *agraphon* (a saying of Jesus not written in the canonical Gospels) found inscribed on a mosque in India and seen in early Islamic writings: "Jesus, on whom be peace, said: 'The world is a bridge. Go over it—do not settle on it!'"

13. Mikhail Lermontov (1814–1841) was a celebrated Russian poet. Father Alexander here mentions Lermontov's poem "The Angel."

14. According to the standard Marxist-Leninist view, any religious tradition or ritual was merely a "survival" of the past that would and should eventually wither away.

15. Eastern Orthodox anthropology sees the human as a psychosomatic being consisting of body and soul. The human spirit is the "eye of the soul" and its highest part, where we discern our communion with God through the Holy Spirit.

16. In the late 1950s, Father Alexander studied biology at the Agricultural Institute in Irkutsk, Siberia.

17. Father Alexander does not mention specific public officials here, but it was commonplace at the time for Soviet citizens to make jokes about Brezhnev's speeches. One example: Brezhnev confronts his speechwriter after he delivers a 45-minute speech, saying that he had requested only a 15-minute speech. The speechwriter replies, "I gave you three copies."

18. In the 1920s, a group called the Renovationists attempted to blend Russian Orthodoxy with Soviet Communism. They only had short-lived support from the Bolsheviks and little to no support from the Orthodox faithful.

19. Hewlett Johnson (1874–1966) visited the USSR on several occasions and was a vocal proponent of communism. His highest position was as the Dean of Canterbury (not to be confused with the Archbishop of Canterbury, the highest position in the Church of England).

20. Gorbachev labeled the Brezhnev era the period of "stagnation." When it came to "heroic acts" of dissidents, however, the state under Brezhnev was far from stagnant, pursuing dissidents by questioning them and sending many to prisons and mental hospitals, with or without trials.

21. Alexis Carrel (1873–1944), a French physician, won the Nobel Prize in Physiology or Medicine in 1912 for pioneering vascular suturing techniques. In 1902, he witnessed the miraculous healing of a woman at Lourdes, a commune in France known for miraculous sightings of Mary. The book Father Alexander cites could be the book *Prayer*, which was translated into English and published in 1946. Carrel is a controversial figure to quote regarding prayer, because he was later a proponent of eugenics and became a regent for the French Foundation for the Study of Human Problems, which conducted eugenics research (and much other useful research) in Nazi-occupied Vichy France.

22. [The saying of this prayer activates powerful psychosocial factors. For this reason, experienced teachers of prayer have forbidden its practice without oversight and spiritual direction. It is especially dangerous when a person stops saying it, which is why a prayer rope is necessary. Say it 50 times, then 50 more, then 100. Those who say the Jesus Prayer as many times as they want without a prayer rope fall under the influence of some kind of uncontrollable psychological state. The Church Fathers, therefore, said that this is a dangerous yet powerful prayer that absolutely requires a living spiritual guide.]

    For more on this prayer, see Chapter Nine.

23. Stories about the Greek mythological figure Orpheus depict him charming and taming wild animals with his music.

24. Father Alexander provides this explanation for Orthodox believers, who are accustomed to the altar being in a sanctuary located behind the iconostasis and accessible only to the clergy.

25. Father Alexander did not give the priest's name, but this is a story that Metropolitan Anthony (Bloom) often recounted. It is Metropolitan Anthony who ascribes this story to Father Jean-Baptiste-Marie Vianney.

26. This is a paraphrase of a story told in various ways by Metropolitan Anthony (Bloom) in his books on prayer. See Metropolitan Anthony of Sourozh, *The Essence of Prayer* (London: Darton, Longman and Todd, 1986), 101, 117, 188–89.

27. For much of the twentieth century, it was illegal to possess a Bible in the Soviet Union, unless one was a clergy member. This did not stop people from smuggling Scriptures in or distributing typed manuscripts of the Bible from person to person. This lecture took place two weeks after Father Alexander coordinated the first meeting of the Russian Bible Society since pre-Soviet times. In 1988 and 1989, the Soviet state allowed over eight million Bibles and New Testaments to be printed, imported, and distributed. Father Alexander's comment here speaks to this context. After decades of no legal access to Scripture, however, the eight million Bibles were far from sufficient for the estimated 72 million Christian believers in the Soviet Union at that time.

28. This is a reference to Saint-Exupery's book *The Wisdom of the Sands*.

29. Father Alexander actually calls these "table legs," but since three-legged, round tables are not commonplace in North America, we have translated this using a typically three-legged piece of furniture.

30. The Scripture passages quoted in the original text (Gen. 2:3; Ex. 23:12) had to do with resting on the seventh day.

31. The phrase here translated as "rat race" is *beg suety* (literally, "running after vanity").

32. Gray slush (Russian: *sliakot*) is common in Russian cities during the spring thaw and after wet snowfalls.

33. In the 1920s, as part of the Bolshevik drive for industrialization and for the eradication of religious observance, the Soviet state instituted a workweek that included Sundays. The implementation of this policy varied regionally and changed periodically, but among most Soviet citizens, Sunday was no longer associated with a day of rest.

34. The Russian term for Sunday, *Voskresen'e*, literally means "resurrection."

35. [Saint Mark the Ascetic, "Directions of St. Mark Extracted from His Other Discourses," in *Early Fathers from the Philokalia: Together with Some Writings of St. Abba Dorotheus, St. Isaac of Syria and St. Gregory Palamas*, selected and trans. from the Russian text *Dobrotolubiye* by E. Kadloubovsky and G. E. H. Palmer (London: Faber and Faber, 1954), 74–75.]

36. Metropolitan Anthony (Bloom) of Sourozh wrote many books specifically on prayer: *Living Prayer* (London: Darton, Longman and Todd, 1966); *School for Prayer* (London: Darton, Longman and Todd, 1970); *God and Man*, with Marghanita Laski (London: Darton, Longman and Todd, 1971); *Courage to Pray*, with Georges LeFebvre (London: Darton, Longman and Todd, 1973). These four books are also published in a collection entitled *The Essence of Prayer* (London: Darton, Longman and Todd, 1986).

37. [Henri Caffarel, *Uroki umnoi molitvy* (*Lessons in Mental Prayer*). Canon Caffarel, currently living in France, leads the spiritual lives of many people in different countries. In a letter to the author, he expressed great joy that the spirit of prayer and the yearning for deeper prayer has not dwindled in the Soviet Union. He gave us his books to use as needed. The main one is called *Lessons in Mental Prayer*, from which many pages below are taken. Although I extensively paraphrase Caffarel, I do not use quotation marks. *Russian editors' note*: We were unsuccessful in finding available copies of this book.]

Canon Henri Caffarel (1903–1996) wrote several works on prayer. The book cited here by Father Alexander is likely Caffarel's *Cinq soirées sur la prière intérieure* (*Five Evenings on Interior Prayer*), which has yet to be translated into English. In all probability, Father Alexander had Caffarel's books translated into Russian. He would have then distributed them among his parishioners in typewritten carbon copies (*samizdat*). This may account for the difficulty the Russian editors had in locating this and other material referenced by Father Alexander.

38. Many Christians work with their spiritual advisors to determine the particular prayer rule they will follow. Father Alexander here is writing as a spiritual advisor to his extended network of new Russian Orthodox believers.

39. [Alexander Elchaninov, *The Diary of a Russian Priest*, trans. Helen Islowsky, prepared by Kallistos Timothy Ware (Crestwood, NY: St. Vladimir's Seminary Press, 2001), 115–16.]

40. [Nicodemus of the Holy Mountain (with Lorenzo Scupoli and Theophan the Recluse), *Unseen Warfare: Being the* Spiritual Combat *and* Path to Paradise *of Lorenzo Scupoli, as edited by Nicodemus of the Holy Mountain and revised by Theophan the Recluse*, trans. from Theophan's Russian text by E. Kadloubovsky and G. E. H. Palmer (London: Faber and Faber, 1963), 151.]

The source to which Father Alexander refers here has a lengthy and complex history of "East meets West." A Roman Catholic monk, Lorenzo Scupoli, first wrote his works *Spiritual Combat* and *Path to Paradise* in Italian in the sixteenth century. These works gained great renown and influenced the work of Saint Francis de Sales. The Greek Orthodox *hesychast* Nicodemus of the Holy Mountain translated Scupoli's works in the late eighteenth century, combining them into one work called *Unseen Warfare*. He provided a relatively faithful translation, but made various modifications (including the addition of further wisdom from the Scriptures and the Church Fathers) to bring the theology in line with Eastern Orthodox thought. He also chose not to reveal the name of the original author, only mentioning that he was "a certain wise man." In the mid-nineteenth century, Theophan the Recluse translated Nicodemus's Greek work into Russian. Whereas Nicodemus made comparatively moderate modifications to Scupoli's text, Theophan took great liberty in his translation, removing entire chapters and replacing them with his own Orthodox understanding of prayer. Additionally, Theophan allows readers to believe that Nicodemus of the Holy Mountain was the original author; hence, Father Alexander attributes Nicodemus here as the author of his source. For the history of this text and its modifications, see H. A. Hodges, "A History of Unseen Warfare," in *Unseen Warfare*, 225–81.

41. [Tikhon of Zadonsk, "Plot' i dukh" ("Flesh and Spirit"), in *Tvoreniia izhe vo sviatykh otsa nashego Tikhona Zadonskogo, episkopa Voronezhskogo* (*The Works of the Saints: Our Father Tikhon of Zadonsk, Bishop of Voronezh*), 4th book (St. Petersburg: 1907), 89.]

42. [Saint Theophan the Recluse, *Pis'ma k raznym litsam* (*Letters to Various Figures*), (no publication information provided), 392. *Russian editors' note*: We have been unsuccessful in locating this text.] Here, Father Alexander and Saint Theophan place themselves firmly in one camp of the ongoing debate in the Orthodox Church over the acceptable frequency of Communion. For a historical overview of this debate

on Mount Athos, see Hieromonk Patapios and Archbishop Chrysostomos, *Manna from Athos: The Issue of Frequent Communion on the Holy Mountain in the Late Eighteenth and Early Nineteenth Centuries*, Byzantine and Neohellenic Studies 2, ed. Andrew Louth and David Ricks (Bern: Peter Lang, 2006).

43. [Nicodemus of the Holy Mountain [with Scupoli and Theophan], *Unseen Warfare*, 153.]

44. [Theophan the Recluse, *Pis'ma*, 289.]

45. [Bishop Ignatius Brianchaninov, "O molitve" ("On Prayer"), in *Sochineniia episkopa Ignatiia Brianchaninova* (*The Works of Bishop Ignatius Brianchaninov*), 4 vols. (St. Petersburg: 1905), 149–50.]

46. [A. K. Tolstoi, *Polnoe sobranie sochineniia* (*Complete Collection of Works*), 4 vols. (St. Petersburg: 1905), IV:40–41.]

    The Russian poet, novelist, and playwright Alexei Konstantinovich Tolstoy (1817–1875) is not to be confused with the famous author Lev (Leo) Tolstoy, who was actually excommunicated from the Russian Orthodox Church for his unique religious views. The two authors were second cousins.

47. [Nicodemus of the Holy Mountain [with Scupoli and Theophan], *Unseen Warfare*, 153.]

48. [Saint Theophan the Recluse, *The Spiritual Life and How to be Attuned to It*, trans. Alexandra Dockham (Forestville, CA: St. Herman of Alaska Brotherhood, 1995), 45.]

49. [*Russian editors' note*: Anthony (Bloom), Metropolitan of Sourozh, is cited here without mention of the source.]

    The metropolitan says something very similar (but not exactly the same) in his book *Living Prayer*. See Metropolitan Anthony of Sourozh, *Essence of Prayer*, 76–77.

50. The term translated here as *negligence* may be referring to the passion known to the Greek Fathers as *acedia* (the absence or lack of care). Through the centuries, this passion has become known as *sloth*, one of the seven deadly sins. Yet, recent scholarship has shown that *acedia* had a much deeper meaning than mere laziness. For more on this, see Kathleen Norris, *Acedia & Me: A Marriage, Monks, and a Writer's Life* (New York: Riverhead Books, 2008).

51. [The Venerable Abba Isaiah, "Slova k svoim emu uchenikam" ("Words to His Followers"), in *Dobrotoliubie*, I:290.]

    The editor could not locate an English translation of this text in any available translation of the *Philokalia* or *Dobrotoliubie*.

52. [*Russian editors' note*: Metropolitan Philaret (Drozdov) is cited here without mention of a specific source.]

53. [For example, see the Monks Callistus and Ignatius, "Directions to hesychasts, in a hundred chapters," in *Writings from the Philokalia-on Prayer of the Heart*, trans. from the Russian text *Dobrotolubiye* by E. Kadloubovsky and G.E.H. Palmer (London: Faber and Faber, 1951), 192–93.]

54. [Archpriest A. V. Men', *Pravoslavnoe bogosluzhenie: Tainstvo, Slovo i Obraz*, (*The Orthodox Liturgy: Mystery, Word, and Image*) (Moscow: Ferro-Logas, 1991), 168–69.] This book has yet to be translated into English.

55. [Saint Mark the Ascetic, "Nastavlenie o dukhovnoi zhizni" ("Instructions on the

Spiritual Life"), in *Dobrotoliubie*, 4th ed., 5 vols. (Moscow: (no publisher listed), 1905), I:514.]

The editor could not locate an English translation of this text in any available translation of the *Philokalia* or *Dobrotoliubie*.

56. [Holy Fathers Barsanuphius and John, "Directions in Spiritual Work," in *Writings from the Philokalia*, 367.]

57. [Anthony (Bloom), Metropolitan of Sourozh, *Pervaia beseda o molitve* (*An Initial Conversation about Prayer*). *Russian editors' note*: We were unsuccessful in locating this text.]

58. Here, Father Alexander may be speaking to a very specific cultural phenomenon of romance novels, similar to the Harlequin Romance series, in Russia. A large portion of women in the Soviet Union and now in post-Soviet Russia have read these books, which are available everywhere. Yet, he chose not to mention romance novels specifically, because that is not the only kind of literature to avoid. He is likely also referring to any kind of literature that stimulates the reader, romantically or otherwise. This might include political material or other controversial material that could make the reader angry, frustrated, excited, etc.

59. [Saint Theodoros the Great Ascetic, "A Century of Spiritual Texts," in *The Philokalia: The Complete Text*, compiled by St. Nikodimos of the Holy Mountain and St. Makarios of Corinth, 4 vols., trans. and ed. G.E.H. Palmer, Philip Sherrard, Kallistos Ware (London: Faber and Faber, 1979–1995), II:29.]

60. [The Venerable Symeon the New Theologian, *Slova* (*Discourses*) (Moscow: (no publisher listed), 1890), 185.]

61. [See Archimandrite Sophrony, *Saint Silouan the Athonite*, trans. Rosemary Edmonds (Crestwood, NY: St Vladimir's Seminary Press, 1999), 269–91.]

62. [Starets Makarius of Optina, *Pis'ma* (*Letters*) (no publishing information provided), 396. *Russian editors' note*: We were unsuccessful in locating this text.]

It is unclear from the Russian original whether Father Alexander added the parenthetical note "(distraction)," or whether it was part of the source he was citing.

63. [Theophan the Recluse, *Pis'ma*, 128.]

64. [Sometimes, the sin of being hard-hearted can be overcome by the thoughtful recitation of the Lord's Prayer, by reading a certain prayer two or three times, or by repeating one cycle of the Jesus Prayer on a prayer rope.]

65. [Saint Francis de Sales, *Rukovodstvo k blagochestivoi zhizni* (*Introduction to the Devout Life*) (Brussels: [La Vie avec Dieu], 1967), 138.]

Another English translation of this passage is found in Saint Francis de Sales, *Introduction to the Devout Life*, trans. John K. Ryan (New York: Harper & Bros., 1950), 208. In the late 1950s, Father Alexander found a French edition of *Introduction to the Devout Life* by Saint Francis de Sales. Father Alexander's beloved "aunt" (Vera Vasilevskaia, actually his mother's cousin) translated it. In 1966, Father Alexander met a woman named Anastasiia (Asya) Duroff (1907–1999), a Russian émigré who worked at the French embassy in Moscow. She had connections with the Catholic publisher La Vie avec Dieu in Belgium. During his conversation with Duroff, Father Alexander told her of the pressing need for religious books in the USSR. Then, or soon thereafter, he handed Duroff his aunt's Russian translation of *Introduction to the Devout Life*. La Vie avec Dieu published it in 1967, and this became his first successful attempt at *tamizdat* (publishing texts abroad and then having them smuggled back in for distribution). La Vie avec Dieu became the main publisher of Father Alexander's works for the next two decades.

66. The writer of *The Shepherd of Hermas* is not known. In several Christian circles, however, the author of the work often came to be known as "Hermas," or "the Shepherd of Hermas."

67. Wednesdays and Fridays are days of fasting in the Orthodox Church.

68. This is a reference to the Liturgy: "We commend ourselves and each other and all our life unto Christ our God." This statement is spoken at the end of each litany.

69. [Examples of meditative phrases include: (a) "has shone to the world the Light of wisdom" (from the Nativity Troparion), (b) "Glory to Thee who has shown us the light" (the Great Doxology from Matins), (c) "Who for us and for our salvation" (from the Nicene Creed), (d) "Come and abide in us" (from "O Heavenly King"), (e) "Let my prayers rise before you" (from the Psalms and Vespers), (f) "And I will give you rest" (Matthew 11:28), and (g) "Open to me the doors of repentance" (from the Canon of Andrew of Crete).]

70. [A. V. Men, *Tainstvo, Slovo i Obraz*, 140–42.]

71. [One example from sacred history would be the Gospel portrayal of Jesus walking on water (Matt. 14:25–33; Mk. 6:45–52; John 6:15–21).]

72. Metropolitan Anthony provides commentary on certain Gospel themes for meditation in his *Meditations on a Theme: A Spiritual Journey* (London: Continuum, 2003).

73. [See Chapter Five about checking yourself in certain spiritual experiences. Most Eastern ascetics consider the element of imagination to be completely incompatible with spiritual meditation. In the West, the element is allowed, and is sometimes recommended. This disagreement came about in ancient times. It is connected to the differences in the psychology of the people in the West and East. The East is more likely to invent and fantasize with very rich imaginations and therefore must receive the antidote in the form of a prohibition to give will to the imagination. The West is more sober and rational needing the opposite—the animation of the spirit with the help of the soul. In our time, these psychological differences have evened out. Therefore, when choosing a method of meditation, more attention should be paid to a person's individual characteristics.]

74. In most Russian Orthodox churches, there are no pews, but people stand throughout the service. Sometimes benches are provided along the back row for those who are unable to stand for long periods of time.

75. [Archpriest R. Putiatin, *Sobranie pouchenii* (Collection of Sermons), ({Russia}: {no publisher listed}, 1893), 99. *Russian editors' note*: We were unable to locate this source.]

76. [Alexander Elchaninov, *Diary of a Russian Priest*, 83.]

77. [Saint John of Karpathos, "For the Encouragement of the Monks in India Who had Written to Him: One Hundred Texts," in *The Philokalia*, I:319–20.]

78. [Metropolitan Anthony of Sourozh, *Essence of Prayer*, 108.]
    This is from his book *Living Prayer*.

79. [Metropolitan Anthony of Sourozh, *Essence of Prayer*, 86.]
    This is from his book *Living Prayer*.

80. [P. Velichkovskii, *Ob umnoi ili vnutrennei molitve* (*On Mental or Interior Prayer*), 4th ed. (Moscow, (no publisher listed), 1912), 38.]
81. [Saint Diadochos of Photiki, "On Spiritual Knowledge and Discrimination: One Hundred Texts," in *The Philokalia*, I:270.]
82. [Nicodemus of the Holy Mountain [with Scupoli and Theophan], *Unseen Warfare*, 160.]
83. Throughout this book, Father Alexander claims that more recent saints like Nicodemus of the Holy Mountain were Church Fathers. To Catholic and Protestant thinkers, it would seem strange to include anyone beyond the eighth century (and, for some, the fifth century) as a Church Father. For some Eastern Orthodox, however, although the early Church Fathers have great significance, the age of the Church Fathers continues. Thus, Father Alexander is reflecting a wider historical conception of the term, bestowing it upon men of great ascetical wisdom in later generations.
84. [Nicodemus of the Holy Mountain [with Scupoli and Theophan], *Unseen Warfare*, 161.]
85. [*Russian editors' note*: Metropolitan Anthony (Bloom) of Sourozh is cited here without mention of a source.]
    The editor could not locate this statement in any of Metropolitan Anthony's books on prayer.
86. [The words of the prayer are recorded accurately enough in the poetry of Alexander Sergeeivich Pushkin. In the translation from the Syriac language, it sounds similar to the Slavonic.]
87. Again, by the word here translated *sloth*, Saint Ephrem likely meant *acedia*. See note 50.
88. Father Alexander was giving an extemporaneous lecture when he spoke these words, and he did not quite recall Saint Seraphim's words correctly. Seraphim actually said, "We must not despair, because Christ conquered all—He raised Adam, freed Eve, and defeated death."
89. The term here translated *humility* is the archaic Russian term *smerenomudrenie*, the roots of which include both humility and wisdom.
90. Ivan Andreevich Krylov (1769–1844) was a well-known Russian literary figure, famous for fables. Krylov adapted the story "The Frog and the Ox" from an Aesopian fable that Jean de La Fontaine (1621–1695) had previously adapted. This fable describes a frog that becomes envious of an ox. In an attempt to become like the ox, the frog puffs himself up until he bursts.
91. In Soviet times, the Russian term used here (*primirenchestvo*) denoted a dangerous reconciliation with a class enemy.
92. The Orthodox calendar consists of several Lenten periods, including the Nativity Fast (six weeks), the Apostles' Fast (one day to five weeks, depending on where Pentecost falls), and the Dormition Fast (two weeks). Therefore, what Western Christians refer to as Lent is called Great Lent in the Eastern Church.
93. According to his spiritual children, Father Alexander himself wrote this prayer.
94. [For example, see the works of Albert Camus and Franz Kafka.]

95. Father Alexander is here referring to the "Fifth Meditation" of Saint Francis de Sales. In this meditation, the saint provides a list of personal questions and considerations for a person who imagines that he is incurably ill on his deathbed, with the purpose of becoming more resolute in his obedience to Christ. See Saint Francis de Sales, *Introduction to the Devout Life*, trans. and ed. John K. Ryan (New York: Harper and Brothers, 1950), 21–22.

96. This week is also called Passion Week.

97. Here, Father Alexander specifically recommends the writings of Innocent of Kherson, Frederic W. Farrar, and J. Cunningham Geikie. These three authors each wrote lives of Christ. Two are available in English, but have been long out of print: Frederic W. Farrar, *The Life of Christ* (New York: Dutton, 1885); J. Cunningham Geikie, *The Life and Words of Christ* (New York: Alden, 1886). Father Alexander dedicated many years to writing *Syn Chelovecheskii (The Son of Man)*, a life of Christ for the Russian-speaking world. In his research for this book, he found great insight from these authors. He wrote brief biographies for each of them in his *Bibliologicheskii Slovar' (Dictionary of Biblical Scholarship)*, which he labored over in the 1980s, during a period of intense oppression from state authorities.

98. Praying with the communion of saints is part of many Christian traditions. For those from the Protestant tradition who want to learn more about this practice, see Jon M. Sweeney, *The Lure of the Saints: A Protestant Experience of Catholic Tradition* (Brewster, MA: Paraclete Press, 2005). For a historical and theological understanding of the Orthodox Church and its practice (including its view of saints), see Timothy Ware, *The Orthodox Church*, new ed. (New York: Penguin Putnam, 1997); Father Alexander Schmemann, *For the Life of the World: Sacraments and Orthodoxy*, 2d ed. (Crestwood, NY: St. Vladimir's Seminary Press, 1973).

99. During Soviet times, the community Sergiev Posad, where the Trinity Saint Sergius Monastery (one of the main centers for Orthodox faith in Russia) is located, was renamed Zagorsk in 1930, in memory of Vladimir Zagorskii, a Bolshevik revolutionary. It now retains its original name. For more on the Trinity Saint Sergius Monastery, where the Moscow Theological Academy is located, see Scott Kenworthy, *The Heart of Russia: Trinity-Sergius, Monasticism, and Society after 1825* (Oxford: Oxford University Press, 2010).

100. Father Alexander is likely referring to the painting *The Last Minutes of Philip II, Metropolitan of Moscow*, which is now displayed at the State Russian Museum in St. Petersburg. Aleksandr Nikanorovich Novoskol'tsev (1853–1919) produced the painting in the 1880s. In the 1960s and early 1970s, Father Alexander often took parishioners to the Moscow Theological Academy and the churches of the monastery to show them old icons and spiritual works of art, many of which were not on display but were in storage for safekeeping.

101. This statement, which originates from Galatians 3:27, is a phrase from the Liturgy used at baptisms and at high holy days in the Orthodox tradition.

102. This is a paraphrase of Saint Ignatius of Antioch's letter to the Ephesians, which he wrote while on his way to Rome, where he was martyred.

103. In the Russian Bible, Jesus calls Himself "the Light to the world" in John 8:12.

104. Tikhon of Zadonsk was inspired to write his book *On True Christianity* after

reading the book *True Christianity* by Johann Arndt (1555–1621), a Lutheran theologian. Arndt's book also inspired German Pietists in the eighteenth century.

105. Sources: *Practical Guide to Prayer* (2nd ed., 1995), and "Iz molitvennogo opyta ottsa Aleksandra" (from Father Alexander's Experience of Prayer, http://www .alexandrmen.ru/fam/pan.html, accessed October 12, 2013).

106. This prayer has started to be included in various Russian collections of prayers, sometimes unattributed.

107. The expression translated here as "everything else will fall into place" is a direct quote from Matthew 6:33, "and all these things shall be added to you." Russian Christians would understand this Scriptural allusion in this context more readily than our English Bible translations would allow.

108. More of Father Alexander's Paschal sermons are available in the book *Awake to Life* (see Recommended Reading).

109. This could also be translated *the gift of the tongue,* but not *the gift of tongues.*

110. Source: "Neopublikovannye prilozheniia k 'Prakticheskomu rukovodstvu k molitve'" (The Unpublished Appendices to *A Practical Guide to Prayer*), http://www.alexandrmen .ru/fam/pan.html, accessed October 12, 2013.

111. This is a reference to the prayer before Communion within the Orthodox Liturgy.

112. [Saints Basil the Great and Maximus the Confessor were among those who advocated frequent communion.]
    See note 42 regarding the debates concerning frequent Communion.

113. [The Orthodox Church acknowledges the validity of the sacrament of Eucharist performed by a properly ordained priest of another confession (Catholic or Old Believer). The fact that we Orthodox Christians do not commune together with them is not because we deny the authenticity of their liturgy, but because of the understanding that this is a feast of love. To take Communion together will only be possible when we achieve unity and end all division. Until that time, taking Communion would be insincere and thus unworthy. But in cases of necessity, as decreed in 1969 by the Holy Synod of the Russian Orthodox Church, Old Believers and Catholics may confess and take Communion in Russian Orthodox churches.]

114. The custom in the Orthodox Church has been to make sure that *Pascha* falls on the first Sunday after the first full moon and after the vernal equinox (according to the Julian calendar), as long as the Jewish Passover is completed.

115. Source: "Prigotovlenie k ispovedi" ("Preparation for Confession"), http://www .alexandrmen.ru/fam/pan.html, accessed October 12, 2013.

116. Bishop Seraphim (Sigrist), "Fr. Men, Fr. Bown and the Detectives," The Alexander Men Conference in Moffat, Scotland (September 15, 2012).

Akathist: A hymn with twenty-four stanzas that is sung to a saint or to Christ, and often at Salutation Services dedicated to the **Theotokos** at Compline on the Fridays of Great Lent.

Analoy: (Greek, *Analogion*). A small table that holds the Gospels, or an icon or cross. It is used in services of marriage and baptism, and during private confession.

Askesis: An exercise of self-discipline for a spiritual purpose. *Askesis* is the Greek word from which the term *asceticism* is derived.

Beatitudes: The ninefold blessing of Christ within the Sermon on the Mount (Matt. 5:3–12). In Orthodox spirituality, the Beatitudes are used as a standard against which a person's current spiritual state can be assessed.

Bishop: (Greek, *Episkopos, Archiereas*). A clergyman in the highest of the sacred orders. A bishop is considered a successor to the apostles. In the Orthodox Church, whereas parish priests are typically married, only celibate clergy may become bishops.

Bright Week: (Greek, *Diakaimsimos*). The week following the Sunday of Easter (*Pascha*), also known as Eastertide.

Canon of Andrew of Crete: A cycle of poetic hymns and prayers used at times during Great Lent in the Eastern rite.

Carmelites: The short name for the monastic Order of the Brothers of Our Lady of Mount Carmel. The order, which emphasizes contemplative prayer, is said to have begun in the twelfth century in Jerusalem, and it continues to this day.

Church Fathers: (Greek, *Pateres*). Great theologians, sometimes known as *patristics*, who lived predominantly in the first five to eight centuries of Christianity. The patristic period is conventionally closed with Saint Gregory Palamas in the East, but some in the Orthodox Church occasionally consider later influential writers to be Church Fathers.

Deacon: The first of the three sequential orders of priesthood (deacon, priest, bishop). A deacon assists the bishop and priest, leads the faithful in prayer, and reads the Gospel. He does not preside over the Eucharist, give blessings, or pronounce absolution.

Divine Liturgy: *Liturgy* means the public duty or work of God's people, an act of worship. The Divine Liturgy is the Eucharistic service of the Orthodox Church served every Sunday and feast day.

Dobrotoliubie: (literally, "love of good") The name of the Slavonic and Russian translations of parts of *The Philokalia*.

Dormition Fast: A two-week fast in preparation for the Feast of the Dormition (i.e., Assumption, or "Falling Asleep") of the **Theotokos** on August 15.

Epiphany: (Greek, *Theophania*; Slavonic, *Bogoiavlenie*). The Orthodox feast that commemorates Christ's baptism (January 6).

Epitrachilion: The liturgical vestment worn by an Orthodox priest or bishop, equivalent to the Western stole. An Orthodox priest must wear this particular vestment to perform a sacrament.

Great Friday: The Friday of Holy Week, called Good Friday in the Western Church.

Great Thursday: The Thursday of Holy Week, called Maundy Thursday in the Western church.

Hesychasm: (Greek, "to be quiet") An ancient Christian spiritual movement that stresses silence, prayer (particularly the Jesus Prayer), meditation, and spiritual exercises as a way to grow in union with God (*theosis*, or *deification*). In the fourteenth century, the movement developed further under the influence of Gregory Palamas on Mount Athos and is practiced to this day.

Hieromartyr: A bishop or priest who has been martyred, dying for his faith.

Holy Mysteries/Holy Gifts: The sanctified wine and bread utilized during the Divine Liturgy.

Holy Synod: In the Eastern Church, a synod is an assembly of the bishops in any local (diocesan) or national unit. In imperial Russia, the Holy Synod existed from 1721 to 1917, designed to oversee the Russian Orthodox Church. After World War II, the Holy Synod re-emerged as the highest governing body of the Church, led by the Patriarch of Moscow.

Hours: In monasteries, monks hold short services for the main hours of the day. The first hour (6:00 AM) focuses on thanksgiving for the morning and prayer for a sinless day; the third hour (9:00 AM) celebrates the descent of the Holy Spirit on Pentecost; the sixth hour (12:00 noon) commemorates the nailing of Christ to the Cross; the ninth hour (3:00 PM) commemorates the death of Christ.

Icon: (Greek, "image") A representation of Christ, the Virgin Mary, other saints, or biblical scenes on wood, canvas, paper, or a wall. The Orthodox Church venerates those depicted on the icon, seeing them as a window to the worship of the Incarnate Christ.

Iconostasis: (Greek, "icon stand") The screen covered with icons that stands between the altar and the nave in an Orthodox Church. The iconostasis has three points of entry: the central Holy Doors (or Royal Gates) and two side doors.

Kukol: The cowl (monastic hood) worn by monks of the Great Schema, the highest degree of monasticism in the Eastern Church.

Lent: A period of prayer and fasting in preparation for a major Church feast. In the Orthodox Church, there are five Lenten periods. Great Lent and Holy Week are the Lenten periods most commonly associated with the Western "Lent," falling before the celebration of *Pascha*.

Litany: A responsive prayer led by a priest or deacon. The congregation responds with "Lord, have mercy" or "Grant this, O Lord." Nearly all Orthodox services contain multiple litanies chanted in the midst of various **troparia**, psalms, or other scriptural readings.

Matins: (Greek, *Orthros*) The morning prayer service.

Metropolitan: Generally, the bishop of a major city (*metropolis*) or province. In Russia, the metropolitan oversees a larger area.

Old Believers: The name of a religious group that originated when they split from the Russian Orthodox Church in 1666 in protest against certain liturgical reforms imposed by Patriarch Nikon.

Pascha: (Greek, from Hebrew *Pesach*, or Passover) The Feast of the Resurrection of Christ, or "the Feast of Feasts." Known as *Easter* in the Western tradition.

Passions: To the church fathers and subsequent Orthodox thinkers, the passions are considered human appetites or urges that can easily lead to sin if not controlled or submitted to God's will.

Patriarch: (Greek, "in charge of the family") The presiding bishop of a national church.

The Philokalia: (Greek, "love of beauty") A collection of texts written by ascetics from the fourth to the fifteenth centuries. Many of the texts discuss the *hesychastic* prayer of the heart, or interior prayer. Saints Nikodemos of the Holy Mountain and Makarios of Corinth compiled this collection in the eighteenth century.

Prayer Rope: (Russian, *chotki*) A circular chord of one hundred knots or beads used to mark the number of repetitions of the Jesus Prayer. It serves a similar purpose to a rosary in the Catholic tradition, or prayer beads in the Anglican tradition.

Prayer Rule: Simply speaking, this is a commitment to pray specific things at a specific, regular time. Certain communities may follow a joint prayer rule. Individuals in the Catholic and Orthodox

Churches often determine their particular prayer rule with the assistance of their spiritual director.

Prosphora: (Greek, "offering gift, an item dedicated to God and offered as a votive") The leavened altar bread specially prepared with pure wheat flour and used for the Divine Liturgy. This blessed bread is received after communion as a symbol of the ancient agape feasts.

Sacrament: (Greek, *Mysterion;* Slavonic, *Tainstvo*) A means of grace. In the Orthodox Church, although seven sacraments are practiced as outward and visible signs, the entire life of the Church is considered mystical (or sacramental).

Saint: (Greek, *Hagios*) Literally, "a holy person." While all Christians are called to be saints (Rom. 16:2; 1 Cor. 1:1–2), the ancient Church started designating certain holy men, women, and angels as saints, due to their pure and holy life on earth or their martyrdom and confession of faith. Believers in the Catholic and Orthodox traditions, and some in the Anglican tradition, continue to venerate saints and ask them to pray for them.

Saint's Day: The day in the Christian calendar on which a particular saint is commemorated. According to tradition, Orthodox people celebrate their name-days on the day when the saint after whom they are named is commemorated.

Starets: (fem. *staritsa,* pl. *startsy*) A person, usually a monk or nun, whom laypeople consult for spiritual direction due to his or her holiness and gifts of spiritual discernment. This has a long tradition in the Greek Church; in Russia, the *startsy* tradition flourished in the nineteenth century, centered around the monastery Optina Pustin.

Tabernacle: (Greek, *Artophorion;* Slavonic, *Darokhranitelnitsa*). A receptacle, sometimes elaborately decorated, that stands on the altar table and contains the Holy Gifts of the Eucharist that are reserved for the Communion of the sick or for the Liturgy of the Presanctified Gifts during Lent.

Theophany: (called "Epiphany" by the Western Church) A manifestation of God in His uncreated glory (e.g., Gen. 18:1–15; 28:10–17). The revelation of the Holy Trinity at Christ's baptism is considered the greatest theophany and is celebrated in the Orthodox Church on January 6.

Theotokos: (Slavonic, *Bogoroditsa*) Literally, "the God-Bearer," and frequently translated "Mother of God." A theological term used by the Orthodox Church to indicate the significance of the Virgin Mary as the mother of Christ.

Troparion: (pl. *troparia*) The name used for several types of short hymns, the most common being the *apolytikion*, which signifies the particular occasion being celebrated on a given day. This term corresponds to the Western term *collect*.

Vespers: (Greek, *Esperinos*; Slavonic, *Litiya*) The evening prayer service.

Xerophagy: The type of fasting that restricts food to "dry eating," which means only raw or cooked vegetables without oil.

GLOSSARY OF IMPORTANT FIGURES

Church Fathers and Christian leaders, saints, and ascetics mentioned or cited by Father Alexander (alphabetical order by first name).

Father Alexander Elchaninov (1881–1934) was a Russian intellectual who left Russia in 1921 in the aftermath of the Bolshevik Revolution and the subsequent Civil War. He was ordained as an Orthodox priest in France in 1926 and became one of the leaders of the Russian Student Christian Movement. Father Sergius Bulgakov (1871–1944) was his mentor. He did not write any books, but left behind his personal notes, which were later published as *The Diary of a Russian Priest*.

Metropolitan Anthony (Bloom) of Sourozh (1914–2003) was the founder and head of the Russian Orthodox Church's Diocese for Great Britain and Ireland. He wrote several books, at least four of which were specifically about prayer.

Saints Barsanuphius and John (6th century) were the Egyptian hermit Barsanuphius of Palestine (or Gaza) and John the Prophet, who was the abbot of the monastery in Merosala. Their joint instructions to monastics are preserved in *The Philokalia*.

Saint Basil the Great (4th century) was the influential Bishop of Caesarea Mazaca. Later generations would call him, his brother Gregory of Nyssa, and Gregory of Nazianzus the Cappadocian Fathers (after the part of Asia Minor where they originated). Basil the Great is best known for three things: his theological stance against the Arian heresy and for the Nicene Creed, his care for the poor and sick, and the development of communal monastic guidelines.

Saints Callistus and Ignatius (14th century) were Callistus I of Constantinople and Ignatius of Xanthopoulos. Callistus I, a disciple of **Gregory Palamas**, was the patriarch of Constantinople from 1350 to 1353 and again from 1354 to 1363. Ignatius seems to only be known for compiling a guide for ascetics along with Callistus I. This guide was later included within *The Philokalia*.

Blessed Diadochos of Photiki (5th century) was an ascetic and the Bishop of Photiki (Greece). His writing, which has been preserved in *The Philokalia*, was influential on several later Byzantine saints and on the *hesychast* (silent monk) movement.

Saint Ephrem of Syria (4th century) was a theologian and hymnographer and is known as the most significant of all Syriac-speaking Church Fathers.

Saint Francis de Sales (1567–1622) was the Roman Catholic Bishop of Geneva (a city led by Calvinists) at a time when religious divisions were occurring all around him in the wake of the Protestant Reformation. He is best known for his writings *Introduction to the Devout Life* and *Treatise on the Love of God*.

Dean Frederic W. Farrar (1831–1903) was a cleric in the Church of England, who eventually became the Dean of Canterbury (Canterbury Cathedral). He wrote many scholarly books on biblical exegesis and on Christ and the apostles.

Saint Gregory Palamas (1296–1359) was a monk on Mount Athos and Archbishop of Thessaloniki. He is best known for his teaching and defense of the ancient practice of interior prayer (*hesychasm*, or "the prayer of the heart").

Canon Henri Caffarel (1903–1996) was a French Catholic monk priest who led a spiritual community focused on the strengthening of marriage and on prayer.

Hermas (1st or 2nd century) is the name of the main character of an early Christian writing called *The Shepherd of Hermas*. In the writing, Hermas (a former slave) is given five visions, which are then followed by twelve mandates and ten parables. This writing was so highly respected by some of the early Church Fathers that they considered it part of the canon of Scripture.

Saint Ignatius Brianchaninov (1807–1867) was a Russian Orthodox bishop who wrote many works on prayer and the spiritual life.

Archbishop Innocent of Kherson (1800–1857) is sometimes called the "Russian Chrysostom" for his preaching. He was a scholar and teacher, as well as a prominent leader within the Russian Orthodox Church in the early nineteenth century. He wrote a life of Christ entitled *The Last Days of the Earthly Life of Our Lord Jesus Christ*.

Abba Isaiah (late 4th century) was a hermit who lived in the desert of Skete in Egypt. His ascetical texts have been passed down in the form of several anecdotes, some of which were preserved within the writings of Saint John of Cassian (c. 360–435).

J. Cunningham Geikie (1824–1906) was a Scottish minister in the Presbyterian Congregationalist Church in Canada. He then became a priest in the Church of England, serving in several parishes in England and France. Later in life, he was in academic administration at Queen's College (Ontario, Canada) and Edinburgh University (Scotland). Geikie's writings included *Hours with the Bible*, *The Life and Words of Christ*, and *The Holy Land and the Bible*. His contemporary Charles Spurgeon described him as "one of the best religious writers of this age."

Saint Jean-Baptiste-Marie Vianney (1786–1859), also known as Saint John Vianney, was the Curé d'Ars (the parish priest in the community of Ars, in eastern France) in the early nineteenth century. He is venerated for revitalizing the Catholic faith in Ars and its surrounding area during the post-Napoleonic period, after the Catholic Church had been significantly deinstitutionalized following decades of revolutionary and post-revolutionary upheaval.

Saint John Climacus (7th century), also known as Saint John of the
Ladder, was a monk at the monastery on Mount Sinai. Very little
is known about this saint, but he left behind a classic devotional
text entitled *The Ladder of Divine Descent*.

Saint John of Karpathos (7th century?) likely came from the island
of Karpathos (between Crete and Rhodes) and may have been the
"John of the island Karpathion" who signed the acts of the Sixth
Ecumenical Council (680–681). One of his writings is preserved
in *The Philokalia*.

Brother Lawrence (c. 1614–1691) was a lay brother in a Carmelite
monastery in Paris. He is best known for his instructions on
interior prayer in the book *The Practice of the Presence of God*.

Starets Macarius of Optina (1788–1860) was one of many well-
respected elders at the Optina Monastery in Russia in the
nineteenth century. He and his fellow elders had not yet been
canonized by the Russian Orthodox Church at the time Father
Alexander was writing.

Saint Mark the Ascetic (5th century) was a disciple of Saint John
Chrysostom (c. 347–407). Some of his writings have been
preserved in *The Philokalia*.

Saint Mary of Egypt (c. 344–421) is the patron saint of penitents.
According to oral tradition, she led a dissolute life as a prostitute
in Egypt for several years before traveling as an "anti-pilgrim" to
Jerusalem. While in Jerusalem, she was convicted of her sin and
after confessing her sin and receiving absolution, she crossed the
Jordan River and lived as a hermit in the desert until her death.

Saint Maximus the Confessor (c. 580–662) was a theologian whose
Christological position against monothelitism (the view that Jesus
has two natures, but one will) was upheld by the third council
of Constantinople, which asserted that Jesus had both divine and
human will.

Saint Nicodemus of the Holy Mountain (c. 1749–1809), also known as Nikodemus the Hagiorite or Nicodemus the Athonite, was a scholar monk best known for his compilation (along with Saint Makarius of Corinth) of *The Philokalia*, a collection of spiritual writings of the Church Fathers.

Saint Paisius Velichkovsky (1722–1794) was a Ukrainian monk who established a hermitage on Mount Athos before relocating to Moldavia to revive monasticism there. He is best known for translating vast amounts of Greek theological texts into Church Slavonic, including parts of *The Philokalia* (called *Dobrotoliubie*), which influenced a later generation of *startsy* (elders) in the Optina Monastery in Russia.

Saint Philaret (Drozdov) (1782–1867) was the Metropolitan of Moscow from 1821 to 1867. He was canonized in 1995, so he was not yet a saint when Father Alexander was writing.

Saint Philip (1507–1569) was the Metropolitan of Moscow from 1566 to 1569. As mentioned by Father Alexander in his sermon (see Chapter Twelve), Saint Philip is venerated for speaking out against the abuses of Ivan the Terrible.

Father Rodion Putyatin (1807–1869) was known for his joyfully humble life. He was greatly respected for being a good preacher, and during his lifetime, his sermons were widely read throughout Russia by people from all walks of life.

Saint Seraphim of Sarov (1754/9–1833) was a Russian monk and mystic. He is now highly renowned for his teaching on prayerful contemplation and on the importance of acquiring the Holy Spirit.

Starets Silouan (1866–1938), also known as Saint Silouan the Athonite, was an Eastern Orthodox monk on Mount Athos in Greece. He was born in Russia, but lived on Mount Athos for the last 45 years of his earthly life.

Saint Symeon the New Theologian (949–1022) was a renowned ascetic. The Eastern Orthodox Church bestowed the name *theologian* upon him at his canonization due to his deep personal experience of God in prayer.

Saint Theodoros the Great Ascetic (9th century), also known as Saint Theodore of Edessa, was a bishop in Syria. He is recognized for having been instrumental in the conversion of Muawid, the "Saracen king," to Christianity. His writings are preserved in *The Philokalia*.

Saint Theophan the Recluse (1815–1894) was a Russian Orthodox bishop and scholar who wrote many devotional works. He is perhaps best known for translating *The Philokalia* (Russian, *Dobrotoliubie*) from Old Church Slavonic into Russian.

Saint Tikhon of Zadonsk (1724–1783) was a Russian Orthodox bishop known for his deep wisdom, holiness, and asceticism.

RECOMMENDED READING

SELECTED WORKS BY FATHER ALEXANDER MEN

About Christ and the Church. Translated by Father Alexis Vinogradov. Torrance, CA: Oakwood Publications, 1996.
  A collection of transcribed "conversations" that took place in the apartments of people in Moscow in the late 1970s and early 1980s.

Awake to Life! Sermons from the Paschal (Easter) Cycle. Foreword by Bishop Seraphim (Sigrist). Translated by Marite Sapiets. Torrance, CA: Oakwood Publications, 1996.
  A collection of transcribed sermons preached by Father Alexander during the season of Great Lent from the late 1970s to the late 1980s.

Christianity for the Twenty-First Century: The Prophetic Writings of Alexander Men. Edited by Elizabeth Roberts and Ann Shukman. New York: Continuum, 1996.
  Selected writings on religion, faith, and Christianity. This book is now out of print, but has recently become available as a Kindle book. Includes a good introduction to Father Alexander Men by Ann Shukman.

Son of Man: The Story of Christ and Christianity. Translated by Samuel Brown. Crestwood, NY: St. Vladimir's Seminary Press, 1998.
  Many consider this work, a Life of Christ, to be Father Alexander's magnum opus.

SELECTED WORKS ABOUT FATHER ALEXANDER MEN

Daniel, Wallace. "Father Aleksandr Men and the Struggle to Recover Russia's Heritage." *Demokratizatsiya* 17, no. 1 (Winter 2009): 73–92.
  Wallace Daniel is currently working on an intellectual biography of Father Alexander. This article will give you a preview of Daniel's upcoming work.

Fr. Alexander Men: The Story of His Life, 1935–1990. Compiled by Father Viktor A. Grigorenko. Translated by Ann Shukman. Moscow: Rudomino, 2012.

This book provides a collection of photographs and quotes that provide a fascinating glimpse into Father Alexander's life and ministry. It may be difficult to obtain in North America.

Hamant, Yves. *Alexander Men: A Witness for Contemporary Russia (A Man for Our Times).* Translated from French by Father Steven Bigham. Torrance, CA: Oakwood Publications, 1995.

The first biography of Father Alexander Men, this work provides a vivid portrait of life for Orthodox believers in the Soviet Union.

Remnick, David. "Black September." In *Lenin's Tomb: The Last Days of the Soviet Empire,* 357–71. New York: Vintage, 1994.

This chapter in a Pulitzer Prize-winning book constitutes a journalist's early appraisal of Father Alexander. Includes a discussion of Father Alexander's unsolved murder and interviews of some of his family and spiritual children.

SELECTED BOOKS ON PRAYER

Anthony (Bloom), Metropolitan of Sourozh. *The Essence of Prayer.* London: Darton, Longman and Todd, 1989.

von Balthasar, Hans Urs. *Prayer.* San Francisco: Ignatius, 1986.

Brother Lawrence. *The Practice of the Presence of God.* Brewster, MA: Paraclete Press, 2010.

Caffarel, Henri. *Being Present to God: Letters on Prayer.* New York: Alba House, 1983.

Foster, Richard. *Prayer: Finding the Heart's True Home.* New York: HarperCollins, 1992.

Mathewes-Green, Frederica. *The Jesus Prayer: The Ancient Desert Prayer That Tunes the Heart to God.* Brewster, MA: Paraclete Press, 2009.

Matthew the Poor. *Orthodox Prayer Life: The Interior Way.* Crestwood, NY: St. Vladimir's Seminary Press, 2003.

Pennington, M. Basil. *Lectio Divina: Renewing the Ancient Practice of Praying the Scriptures.* New York: Crossroad, 1998.

Williams, Rowan. *The Dwelling of the Light: Praying with Icons of Christ.* Grand Rapids, MI: Eerdmans, 2003.

———. *Ponder These Things: Praying with Icons of the Virgin.* Reprint edition. Brewster, MA: Paraclete Press, 2012.

PRAYER BOOKS

Father Alexander frequently mentions praying with a prayer book. Prayer books are available from Orthodox, Catholic, and Anglican/Episcopal churches, all of which utilize specific books of prayer. Several ecumenical versions have recently arisen, with titles such as *Celtic Daily Prayer* and *Common Prayer: A Liturgy for Ordinary Radicals.*

ABOUT PARACLETE PRESS

WHO WE ARE

Paraclete Press is a publisher of books, recordings, and DVDs on Christian spirituality. Our publishing represents a full expression of Christian belief and practice—from Catholic to Evangelical, from Protestant to Orthodox.

We are the publishing arm of the Community of Jesus, an ecumenical monastic community in the Benedictine tradition. As such, we are uniquely positioned in the marketplace without connection to a large corporation and with informal relationships to many branches and denominations of faith.

WHAT WE ARE DOING

Books Paraclete publishes books that show the richness and depth of what it means to be Christian. Although Benedictine spirituality is at the heart of all that we do, we publish books that reflect the Christian experience across many cultures, time periods, and houses of worship. We publish books that nourish the vibrant life of the church and its people—books about spiritual practice, formation, history, ideas, and customs.

We have several different series, including the best-selling Paraclete Essentials and Paraclete Giants series of classic texts in contemporary English; Voices from the Monastery—men and women monastics writing about living a spiritual life today; award-winning poetry; best-selling gift books for children on the occasions of baptism and first communion; and the Active Prayer Series that brings creativity and liveliness to any life of prayer.

Recordings From Gregorian chant to contemporary American choral works, our music recordings celebrate sacred choral music through the centuries. Paraclete distributes the recordings of the internationally acclaimed choir Gloriæ Dei Cantores, praised for their "rapt and fathomless spiritual intensity" by *American Record Guide*, and the Gloriæ Dei Cantores Schola, which specializes in the study and performance of Gregorian chant. Paraclete is also the exclusive North American distributor of the recordings of the Monastic Choir of St. Peter's Abbey in Solesmes, France, long considered to be a leading authority on Gregorian chant.

Video Our videos offer spiritual help, healing, and biblical guidance for life issues: grief and loss, marriage, forgiveness, anger management, facing death, and spiritual formation.

Learn more about us at our website:
www.paracletepress.com,
or call us toll-free at 1-800-451-5006.

SCAN
TO
READ
MORE

YOU MAY ALSO BE INTERESTED IN

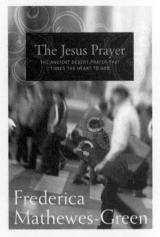

THE JESUS PRAYER

The Ancient Desert Prayer that Tunes the Heart to God

Frederica Mathewes-Green

ISBN: 978-1-55725-659-1   PAPERBACK $16.99

Frederica Mathewes-Green offers the most comprehensive book to date on the Jesus Prayer—a spiritual jewel for anyone who yearns for a real and continuous presence with Christ. She illuminates the history, theology, and spirituality of Orthodoxy, so that the Prayer can be understood in its native context, and provides practical steps for making it a part of our being.

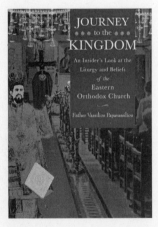

JOURNEY TO THE KINGDOM

An Insider's Look at the Liturgy and Beliefs of the Eastern Orthodox Church

Father Vassilios Papavassiliou

ISBN: 978-61261-164-8   PAPERBACK $18.99

The Orthodox Liturgy is not just an act of worship, but a potentially life-changing journey. Fr. Papavassiliou takes you through this journey with clarity and passion, exploring the Liturgy as a reflection of heavenly worship, and an invitation to enter the Kingdom of God. The hymns, prayers, creed, and actions of the Liturgy are explained, covering subjects such as Communion, Trinity, baptism, sainthood, Resurrection, and much more. The book includes a map and 20 illustrations.

Available from most booksellers or through Paraclete Press:
www.paracletepress.com   1-800-451-5006
Try your local bookstore first.